ZACH

LAMAR

COBB

El Paso Collector of Customs and Intelligence
During the Mexican Revolution
1913–1918

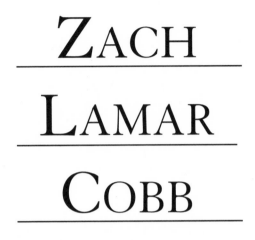

ZACH

LAMAR

COBB

El Paso Collector of Customs and Intelligence

During the Mexican Revolution

1913–1918

JOHN F. CHALKLEY

SOUTHWESTERN STUDIES NO. 103

© 1998
Texas Western Press
The University of Texas at El Paso
El Paso, Texas 79968-0633

First Edition
Library of Congress Catalog No. 96-61730
ISBN 0-87404-199-6

∞

Texas Western Press books are printed on acid-free paper, meeting
the guidelines for permanence and durability of the Committee on
Production Guidelines for Book Longevity of the Council on Library
Resources.

CONTENTS

To my wife, Donna, and daughters,
Marie, Katie, Erin, and especially Zora Lee

ACKNOWLEDGMENTS

Many people and institutions helped me with this project. Particular thanks go to Dr. Ray Sadler for his advice and patience; Drs. Charles Harris and James Matray, who provided inspiration and example as teachers and historians; my parents, who once again sheltered me during a research trip to Washington, D.C., and still have so much to teach me; the library staff at New Mexico State University, especially Don Barclay; archivists at the National Archives and Records Administration, especially Aloha South, who shared their time and patience; friends and relatives, particularly Dr. David Francis, who offered support and understanding; New Mexico State University, which provided me a research grant that made the product much more professional; the Dallas Historical Society for their hospitality; and my four girls, to whom I give special thanks for their patience and quiet time while I worked. A note to Zora Lee, born during this project's long gestation: your initials only coincidentally match Zach Lamar Cobb's. A final acknowledgment to my wife, Donna, for her patience and support. Despite all this help, any errors are entirely and jealously mine; to those noted above goes any credit.

Introduction

THE MEXICAN REVOLUTION (1910–1920) has earned a variety of portrayals and interpretations. Some historians have seen it as a social manifestation of international concepts or as a continuation of the struggle for Mexican independence and identity initiated in 1810. Others have perceived the revolution as a nationalistic expression of sovereignty and a focus of international—particularly Yankee capitalist—intrigue, interference, and intervention in another nation's affairs.[1] Each of these views represents a valid perception of a complex phenomenon from but a single viewpoint. A little-considered vantage point of the Mexican Revolution presents a situation essential to the creation of a U.S. intelligence system. Historians of the development of U.S. intelligence have generally ignored or misinterpreted the Mexican Revolution and its impact along the border. The period as a whole earns little notice, or the coverage concentrates on U.S.-Mexican relations with respect to the European war, German operations in Mexico, the Punitive Expedition, and the Zimmermann telegram.[2] However, the complexities and proximity of the Mexican Revolution, its impact along the border, and policy makers' need for information created a small cottage industry for intelligence agents.

Prominent among the many intelligence agents along the U.S.-Mexican border, because of the number and variety of his reports, political connections, and length of service, stands Zach Lamar Cobb. During a significant portion of the military phase of the Mexican Revolution, he served as the collector of customs for the Port of El Paso (1913–1918) and its surrounding district. From this post, and in addition to his primary duties, he provided numerous reports, analysis, and commentary on contemporary events and potential areas of concern directly to the Department of State. Additionally, when the situation demanded, he took action to influence events. His reports and actions have earned him notice and passing comment from historians of the Mexican Revolution and those of the development of U.S. intelligence. However, no one has undertaken a detailed analysis and examination of his career or performance as collector of customs. This study will fill this historical and analytical void. Cobb represents a transitional figure, from amateur operative to professional agent, in the development of an intelligence capability.

During the period from 1900 to 1920, El Paso transformed itself from a frontier town into a western city. Mining, transportation, commerce, and opportunity, particularly in the form of the Mexican Revolution, all played vital roles in this transformation. Historian W. H. Timmons provides a succinct description of the shift.

> Here was a railroad center with links to the prosperous ranches of Chihuahua and the mines of Sonora and Coahuila; here was a large Mexican population whose loyalties had remained with the land of their birth and who still harbored resentments against the policies of the Díaz regime; here in spite of existing American neutrality legislation was a potential source of arms, munitions, and provisions; here across the river was Ciudad Juárez, with a federal garrison, customhouse, and several banks. As a center and a base for revolutionary operations, therefore, the El Paso–Ciudad Juárez area offered almost unlimited possibilities.[3]

The vibrancy and vitality of the border area also created a rich arena for intelligence operations.

An examination of intelligence's function prior to 1913 enhances an understanding of Cobb's role. Intelligence in its simplest form is information. To a nation, information or knowledge falls easily into two categories: domestic or foreign. The techniques and methods, or tradecraft, of intelligence are similar for both categories, including the intelligence cycle of collection, reporting, analysis, and dissemination. The most essential contribution of intelligence at the national level falls in the area of knowledge of foreign powers. Effective statecraft requires accurate and reliable information on which to base policies ensuring the survival and growth of the state. Intelligence, for this presentation, will highlight foreign over domestic aspects, and collection and reporting of pertinent information over analysis and dissemination. Operations to obtain intelligence take two forms: overt or open and covert or concealed. Overt collection and reporting implies a utilization of public sources ranging from foreign newspapers, popular literature, and published government documents to contacts with government officials and influential citizens conducted openly by both official and private representatives of one nation to another. Covert implies a use of disguised or secret agents to collect and report information obtained through bribery, theft, or unauthorized observation not ordinarily available. Agents, defined as both overt or covert collectors of information, can also be employed to provoke, influence, or control the actions of a foreign nation.

According to Allen Dulles, an early and influential director of Central Intelligence, in the nineteenth and early twentieth century, intelligence:

> was conducted on a fairly informal basis, with only the loosest kind of organization and there is for the historian, as well as the student of intelligence, a dearth of coherent official records. Operations were run out of a general's hat or a diplomat's pocket so to speak.[4]

This generally represents an accurate presentation of intelligence capabilities at the start of the Mexican Revolution. The United States possessed, generously speaking, three intelligence organizations: the Office of Naval Intelligence, established in 1882; an embryonic U.S. Army intelligence capability in the Signal Corps; and the Secret Service of the Treasury Department, primarily concerned with suppression of counterfeiting and presidential security, which occasionally conducted foreign intelligence operations. After its establishment in 1908, the Bureau of Investigation occasionally provided intelligence. Its contribution increased after July 1916 with authorization from Congress to conduct investigations for the Department of State. However, during the early period of the Mexican Revolution all these organizations' contributions to foreign intelligence were limited. Intelligence in support of statecraft and diplomacy fell under the responsibility of State Department diplomats.

Washington's information regarding events in Mexico originated with one central source—U.S. Ambassador to Mexico Henry Lane Wilson. His reporting presented the facts officially available and frequently included a penetrating and insightful analysis of the events and circumstances in Mexico. From June through December 1910, Wilson reported on the popular attitude toward the regime of Porfirio Díaz, as well as the revolutionary movement of Francisco Madero and its suppression based on "verbal official information."[5] His observations and reports formed the basis of President William Howard Taft's response to events in Mexico—waiting, watching, and striving to be on the winning side. As a result of H. L. Wilson's meeting with Taft at the White House in early March 1911, the president ordered the mobilization and movement of one quarter of the U.S. Army to the border and movement of U.S. Navy ships to ports on Mexico's coasts. Taft's purpose, Edward P. Haley writes, was to "strengthen the forces of law and order . . . put both parties on notice in that Republic that we were ready to defend our rights if occasion arose . . . [and to stop] . . . the crossing and recrossing of filibustering expeditions."[6]

As the army formed on the border, intelligence regarding conditions south of the Rio Grande became increasingly vital. To obtain information, two officers, Capts. Paul B. Malone and Charles D. Rhodes, disguised as journalists, moved across the border separately to avoid suspicion, then joined forces at Torreon. The men apparently spoke little if any Spanish, as their primary contacts focused on American and British nationals residing in Mexico. They traveled all the way to Mexico City and returned safely to the United States on October 13, 1911. While theirs was certainly a foreign intelligence mission, their report seems to have had little effect on diplomatic considerations as it does not appear in the relevant files of the State Department. Following such a bold beginning, the army would not reenter Mexico until 1914.[7]

Ambassador Wilson's reports remained the primary source of information on events in Mexico for the U.S. government. For Washington, again according to Haley:

> characteristics that marked Wilson's later political reporting were already in evidence: the situation is defined so that any change, short of the installation of another iron-fisted dictator, is considered dangerous; the telegrams swing wildly from reports of total government success to reports of "serious reverses," and the domestic Mexican political climate is depicted in an ominous light.[8]

Typical of the ambassador's reports to the State Department is one dated November 19, 1910, the day before Madero's planned uprising.

> [Mexican] Government informs me that revolutionary outbreaks Puebla and Juárez yesterday. Situation well in hand and no disturbance elsewhere. Government not as frank as it might be and reports from other sources qualify situation as serious, especially at Puebla, where I have cause to believe about one hundred people killed. The Journal El Pais which continues publishing violent and incendiary articles will be suppressed at my request. WILSON [9]

This telegram, sent in cipher, or code, clearly illustrates Ambassador Wilson's utilization of official sources and interference in local affairs.

Ambassador Wilson's overt reporting from public sources hints at the availability of other sources. Principal among these were the various U.S. consuls throughout Mexico, particularly U.S. Consul Luther T. Ellsworth at the Mexican border town of Ciudad Porfirio Díaz, now Piedras Negras, across from Eagle Pass, Texas.[10] Consuls in this period were a semiautonomous diplomatic organization of the Foreign Service and Department of State. They were political appointees organized in a hierarchy from the consular agent at the base through a supervising regional consul general with links to the ambassador and the State Department. Consuls acted primarily to promote trade and did not enjoy diplomatic immunity.[11] Ellsworth, in 1910, in addition to his regular duties, acted as an agent of the Justice Department coordinating local and federal efforts to maintain a neutrality network along the border. A message to the State Department dated November 19, 1910, illustrates the extent of his network.

> There is evidence on both sides of the border line of serious unrest and intrigue. Have situation on American side of border well in hand and with assistance of federal officers of Customs, Immigration, etc., United States Marshals, Bureau of Investigation Agents, United States Secret Service men, and the United States Cavalry will keep it so. Will not ask for cavalry until necessary but have arranged with the Commander to have them ready to answer my call.[12]

In addition, Ellsworth's reports frequently contrasted with those of H. L. Wilson and formed a second source of information on events:

> Ellsworth's assessment of the situation, relayed to the State Department in late 1910, becomes significant since it differed considerably from information the secretary received from

Ambassador Wilson and from the Mexican government. The Díaz government persisted in its assertion that some connection existed between Flores Magon and the Madero movement. Both Ambassador Wilson and the Mexican government declared the revolution all but ended, while Ellsworth . . . declared it was growing stronger. . . . The conflicting reports no doubt made it difficult for the secretary of state to develop an American policy toward the revolt.[13]

However, in a contest between consul and ambassador, the winner, whose information gains attention and influence, becomes easily apparent. Ellsworth's significance lay in his personal intelligence activities. He stood among the first to report Japanese involvement in the Mexican Revolution, and to coordinate federal officials along the border as a precursor for other consuls and officials. Dorothy Kerig, Ellsworth's chronicler, in her final line assesses Ellsworth succinctly.

Despite his pompousness and his propensity to engage in the work of a sleuth at the expense of his consular duties, Ellsworth submitted a continuing stream of intelligence data to Washington which no doubt helped his government to reach vital decisions on significant matters pertaining to the course of the Mexican Revolution.[14]

Madero's successful occupation of Mexico City between May 1911 and February 1913 represented a return to normal diplomatic and intelligence channels. General Victoriano Huerta's bloody seizure of power in the *decena trágica* (tragic ten days) created unexpected challenges and opportunities for intelligence collection.

Huerta's presidency formed a significant turning point not only in U.S.-Mexican relations but in how the United States collected information. Opposition to Huerta spread throughout Mexico, particularly along the northern border. Dissent shifted the focus of power from a singular location and person to multiple locations and personalities. As the challenge to collect information increased, the ability to collect decreased. President Woodrow Wilson, subsequent to his inauguration on February 12, 1913, refused to recognize the Huerta regime, a significant departure from traditional policy. The result was not only crippling to Huerta but also to the ability of the United States to collect information. For President Wilson, the distrust of Ambassador Wilson, carried over from the Taft administration, became intolerable. Accordingly, President Wilson lacked an impartial and reliable source of information on the situation in Mexico. His policy during the first six months of his administration, Kendrick Clements claims, "was dictated more by instinct than by knowledge."[15]

President Wilson understood his own inherent need for accurate and reliable information. After discussing Mexico with his cabinet, Wilson concluded "that they all lacked trustworthy information upon which to base a policy."[16] At a cabinet meeting of April 18, 1913, "the advisability of sending 'a confidential man' to Mexico to 'study the situation and get exact facts' was one of the topics of discussion."[17] Additionally, at a biweekly press conference Wilson stated, "The trouble is that we don't know what is going on in Mexico."[18] Finally, Wilson wrote to his wife in September 1913, "I do not know what to make of it. The apparent situation changes like quicksilver. But the real situation, I fancy, remains the same, and is likely to yield to absent treatment."[19] Clearly, Wilson appreciated his lack of information and corresponding incomplete understanding of the events in Mexico.

The solution to such a quandary rested within easy reach. President Wilson and the State Department employed a series of 11 agents, according to Larry D. Hill, to obtain information and influence events.

> Wilson sent some of his agents to Mexico on fact-finding missions, and, although their reports were often routed through the Department of State, they were directly responsible to the president. This group included William Bayard Hale, Reginaldo Del Valle, and Duval West. Others were sent to carry on diplomatic relations with the government in Mexico City or with leaders of

the revolutionary factions. John Lind and Paul Fuller were diplomatic agents. Both of them also served as fact finders. Another, David Lawrence, went of his own volition but with the president's blessing, and had only the most tenuous ties to the White House. Others, including George C. Carothers, John R. Silliman, Leon J. Canova and John W. Belt, were State Department agents. Carothers and Silliman served simultaneously as consuls, Belt as a consular secretary, and their salaries were paid by the Consular Service. H. L. Hall was sent to Mexico with only his expenses being paid by the State Department, but his services were terminated before they really began.[20]

Of these 11 men, George C. Carothers achieved distinction as certainly the most controversial and possibly the most effective of Wilson's agents. Despite nearly losing his position as U.S. consul in Torreón in 1912, Carothers continued to serve. He came to the attention of the Wilson administration when he successfully persuaded Mexican revolutionary Francisco (Pancho) Villa not to harm Torreón's resident foreign nationals during Villa's successful attack on that city in October 1913. Based on this accomplishment and an interview in November 1913 with Boaz Long, the State Department's chief of the Division of Latin American Affairs, Carothers became a special agent of the State Department. The following month he received his assignment to influence, control, and report on Villa.[21] Accompanying Villa during his subsequent military operations in northern Mexico, Carothers frequently found himself out of communications with Washington. To rectify this, he made a proposal to Secretary of State William Jennings Bryan.

I wish to state that Mr. Zach L. Cobb, has been of great assistance to me, as *I have consulted everything with him; knowing that you have confidence in his judgment,* I wish to suggest, if it meets with your approval, that I receive and forward instructions and reports while in the interior, through him here [El Paso, Texas]. Villa has offered me the use of his telegraph lines and has told me that I can dispose of special trains or any other means at his disposal, for my messengers. In all events, my reports will have to come here first and I would like them to be forwarded through Mr. Cobb, as I have kept him in close touch with the situation. He is also acquainted with Villa's confidential man, Mr. de la Garza [sic], who will tell Cobb everything, whereas, he might be adverse to giving information to anyone else.[22] (Emphasis added.)

Carothers's proposal brought Cobb into the official family of the Department of State as a mere communications relay point. Cobb's initial service for Carothers and Bryan held influence with low risk and a painless introduction to the opportunity of intelligence. From this meager introduction, Cobb started what became a second career as an *ex officio* intelligence operative in addition to his duties as collector of customs.

CHAPTER ONE

Appointment
and
Transformation

NEITHER COBB'S APPOINTMENT as collector of customs nor Carothers's recommendation of Cobb to Secretary of State Bryan was accidental. Rather, they marked for Cobb recognition of his talents and political activism at the local, state, and national levels. He saw himself as a politician, and his current position resulted from his most daring and successful political efforts to date. Public service and political gain would always remain the bases of Cobb's actions. Future opportunity and promotion would flow from his performance as collector in response to the needs of his political seniors and constituents arising from events of the Mexican Revolution. Cobb's introduction to the functions and possibilities of intelligence occurred within this political context. Family heritage provides the first clues to Cobb's political background, while examination of his accomplishments during his tenure as collector shows his subtle political talents and interest.

Cobb's family background in Georgia presents a strong tradition of involvement in political affairs. Zach Cobb's grandfather, Howell Cobb, Sr., served as:

> Solicitor-General; six times Member of Congress [1843-51 and 1855-57]; Speaker of the United States House of Representatives [1849-51]; Governor of Georgia [1851-53]; Secretary of the Treasury [1857-60]; President of the Provincial Congress of the Confederate States [1861]; Colonel, Brigadier-General and Major General in the Confederate Army.[1]

Additionally, Howell Cobb, Sr.'s, uncle, another Howell Cobb,

> after whom he [Howell Cobb, Sr.] was named, and of whom he was the legatee, was a Member of Congress from Georgia during the War of 1812. Thomas W. Cobb, a cousin and intimate friend of his father, and after whom Cobb county is named, was a Member of Congress from 1817 to 1824, and later United States Senator from Georgia.[2]

Howell Cobb, Sr., lost his family's plantation, Cherry Hill, to Sherman's march through Georgia.[3] The loss of property engendered a consequent respect for property rights which came, as will be seen, to play a role in Cobb's attitude toward personalities and events in Mexico. Howell Cobb, Sr.'s, biographer said of him in summary:

> In a lively public career which spanned more than three decades [Howell] Cobb had traveled almost full circle. Beginning as an obscure though fanatically loyal Democratic congressman during the 1840's, he had quickly risen to a position of vast national power. As a master politician his instinctive shrewdness and his penchant for stealthful machination were matched only by consummate ambition.[4]

The characteristics of stealth, independence, and flexibility, as well as political ambition, would surface once again in the senior Cobb's grandson.

Continuing his political heritage, Zach Cobb's father, Howell Cobb, Jr., served as a member of the Georgia House of Representatives, as did his uncle, John A. Cobb. Another uncle, Andrew J. Cobb, served as an associate justice of the Supreme Court of Georgia. The Lamar side of his family also provided a political heritage through which Cobb could claim a kinship with Mirabeau Lamar, president of the Republic of Texas (1838–1841). Lucius Quintus Cincinnatus Lamar served in the House of Representatives from Mississippi and as the secretary of the interior under President Grover Cleveland, who then nominated him in 1887 for associate justice of the Supreme Court. On confirmation, he sat "as the first Southerner since his own cousin John A. Campbell (1853) and the first Democrat since Stephen J. Field (1862)."[5] Joseph Rucker Lamar served as associate justice of the United States Supreme Court (1911–1916) and acted for his childhood friend, President Woodrow Wilson, as the head of the United States delegation at the Niagara Conference with Mexico, Argentina, Brazil, and Chile in 1914.[6] In recognition of his political lineage, Cobb would describe himself as a "member of a family which had long been active in the political life of not only the state of Georgia but of the nation."[7]

Zach Lamar Cobb, born on January 26, 1880, in Athens, Clark County, Georgia, inherited his name from Zachariah Lamar, his paternal grandmother's father, which underlines the importance of heritage in his family.[8] Provisionally accepted to the United States Military Academy in 1896, he instead attended and graduated from the University of Georgia in 1900. He moved to El Paso in 1901 and established a law office, became active in community affairs, and purchased several hundred acres of land south of El Paso. His interest in politics remained strong but unsatisfied as he unsuccessfully ran for several offices: police judge, office of recorder for the city of El Paso (1903), district attorney (1904), and Congress (1906).[9] In addition to his seemingly perpetual candidacy, his community involvement included organizing a chapter and serving as initial chairman of Sons of Confederate Veterans. And based on his oratory at the 1904 Portland, Oregon, convention, the next American Mining Congress convened at El Paso in November 1905.[10]

His political activism probably earned him the honor of hosting William Jennings Bryan and William Jennings Bryan, Jr., and his wife at an "elaborate eight course dinner" on September 29, 1909, which included R. F. Burges, Millard Patterson, Felix Martinez, Park Pitman, A. Courchesune, and Judge John H. James of San Antonio.[11] The younger Bryan arranged to stay with the Cobbs on a return trip the next month. This in part explains Carothers's allusion in his letter of February 10, 1914, to Bryan's assumed "confidence in his [Cobb's] judgment."[12]

Cobb's real ascent to influence and recognition began in May 1912 at the Texas State Democratic Convention in Houston. He secured for himself, with a "gilt-edged speech," a seat on the Texas delegation to the National Democratic Convention in Baltimore.[13] In the process, he charged the regular delegates from El Paso, particularly State Senator Claude B. Hudspeth, "with being representatives of a corrupt and dishonest political ring," while presenting himself as "the original Wilson man of west Texas."[14] As one of forty Wilson delegates from Texas, Cobb represented a decidedly progressive element in the party. At Baltimore, the Texas delegation would provide vital and decisive support to Wilson.[15] In addition to his service as a delegate, Cobb responded in October to a request from Albert S. Burleson, then in charge of Wilson's speakers' bureau and western headquarters and later his postmaster general, "to join the ranks of the leaders who are conducting the Woodrow Wilson presidential campaign in the west."[16] Cobb stumped in several northern states probably at his own expense using part of the $19,800 he made selling 180 acres below El Paso that same month.[17]

Undoubtedly as a result of his service and associated political connections, particularly with Thomas B. Love who led the Wilson movement in Texas, Cobb earned consideration for appointment to the post of collector of customs in January 1913.[18] Nonetheless, the post would remain contentious for several more

William Jennings Bryan (top rear of the crowd) at El Paso Union Station, El Paso, Texas, possibly in September 1909 for Cobb's dinner party. Cobb is to the right of the trombone behind the drum.
(Courtesy of the El Paso Public Library.)

months. Within Texas, Evan Andres writes, the "customs service remained the most coveted federal patronage prize along the Rio Grande."[19] Political competition for the post increased.

> Having failed to capture what they considered their fair share of the high-level appointments, Texas Wilson men outside the [Col. Edward Mandell] House circle were determined to influence the distribution of postmasterships, collectorships and other federal jobs in their home state.[20]

However, Cobb would not receive the post until September due, from the local perspective, to "Wilson holding up distribution of jobs until he gets the sort of tariff bill he wants within sight of the statute books."[21] Also influencing the decision at the national level loomed the Mexican problem. In Washington, to "ensure the effective enforcement on his [Wilson's] ban against the shipment of munitions into Mexico, the President and his advisors wanted to staff the customs houses along the Mexican border with officials completely loyal to the administration."[22] Finally, on September 24, 1913, Cobb took the oath as collector from his political friend Judge Dan M. Jackson in the presence of other friends, notably Dr. I. J. Bush, and employees of the customs department.[23]

In his $4,500-a-year position as collector, Cobb quickly began to make himself noticed.[24] Through early 1915, in addition to duties in the customs house, communications support for Carothers and occasional reaction or commentary on events characterized Cobb's activities. Marion Letcher, U.S. consul in Chihuahua, in a contemporary account, painted a rather unflattering and unsubstantiated picture of Cobb's performance during the ensuing months. Letcher described Cobb as collecting and reporting to Bryan "all information possible on matters then transpiring in Mexico, since he, Mr. Bryan, was to be secretary of state [sic]."[25] Cobb also "was to be given large powers in an unofficial way in then delicate Mexican embroglio [sic]."[26] Additionally, Cobb's influence with Bryan gained Carothers his initial appointment and instructions "to cooperate with Cobb."[27] Letcher found the ambitious Cobb "not to be venal, but merely a narrow and bigoted enthusiast, carried away with the responsibility suddenly brought to him and made to dream that he might play a part as an empire builder, a great Warwick [sic] in Mexican political affairs" and as a pliant tool for "the interests of the Guggenheims."[28]

Another account of Cobb comes from future brigadier general and military historian S. L. A. Marshall who, then 15 years old, had returned to El Paso in 1915. He observed events along the border until his enlistment in the U.S. Army on November 28, 1917. Marshall knew Zach Cobb's brother, El Paso Deputy Sheriff Howell Cobb, very well and found Zach Cobb to be

a very small man, very slight. He was more birdlike than anything else. . . . terrier like, but that's not true. He was a kinetic, a
very emotional conversationalist and so on and he possessed
considerable intellect. He was a charming companion to be
with. . . . I can't recall his being anti-Villista. He did, due to dint
of circumstance, play major parts [in United States response to
the Mexican Revolution]. But I wouldn't say it was because he
had an anti-Villista attitude. It was because of his job that he
filled at the time. . . . He was not, let me say, an outstanding figure in El Paso circles. His job made him an important figure.
But he was a man who got around a great deal and became a
well known figure in El Paso.[29]

Examination of events, relationships, attitudes, and actions favors
Marshall's picture over that painted in Letcher's account. That Howell Cobb served as a deputy sheriff may serve to explain his brother's
future knowledge of some of the darker aspects of El Paso life.

Zach Cobb's most frequent function, at least for the next several
months and in terms of message count, consisted of acting as
Carothers's communications officer. This had the advantage of allowing him to become aware of Washington's concerns and interests. In
this role Cobb diligently relayed messages, keeping any comments he
occasionally added distinctly separate. Support for Carothers required
relaying his messages, tracking him down in Mexico, and, all too frequently, defending him to Washington. Allegations of personal financial impropriety dogged Carothers.[30] He nevertheless continued in
his duties due to his apparent influence with Villa and because, in
part, he received endorsements from Cobb. In a personal letter to
General Hugh Lennox Scott, Cobb described his situation.

I have gone a long way, perhaps longer than a shrewd politician
would, in praising the work of Carothers to our friends in
Washington because he is the best fitted man I have ever seen
for dealing with the Constitutionalists, both Villa and Carranza,
especially Villa. The real test, of course, is to come when the
plans of the provisional government are submitted to Villa.[31]

Championing Carothers did not necessarily imply seniority in the relationship. Cobb frequently found himself explaining and apologizing for differences to their mutual superiors. For example, in Cobb's first message for the record and foray into diplomacy, he became involved, as a result of a visit from General Luis Terrazas, the prominent Chihuahua landowner and political powerbroker, in trying to resolve Villa's earlier kidnapping of Luis Terrazas, Jr.[32] While the telegram and plea to Bryan had little effect on the situation, Carothers's comment, "Have seen copy of Cobb's telegram relative to Terrazas, Jr., do not think Carranza would take kindly to this as it is entirely Mexican," embarrassed Cobb.[33] In immediate response Cobb defended himself, saying:

> My principal purpose in writing you [Bryan] March fifth was to submit information regarding Terrazas thinking that some day we might have to treat with the Terrazas faction in similar matter. However Carothers is so infinitely your more valuable man in dealing with the constitutionalists his judgment should be considered.[34]

After additional fence mending with Bryan, Cobb still garnered Bryan's recognition when Villa finally resolved the situation in June 1914.[35]

August 1914 proved Cobb's most stressful and busy month to date as an agent and diplomat. Feuding between Villa and Venustiano Carranza, his ostensible superior as the Constitutionalist leader, had caused Cobb, Carothers, and Bryan concern for several months.[36] Nonetheless, on August 1, Carothers arrived in Washington to defend himself from yet another series of corruption charges including some from Carothers's newly appointed assistant, Leon J. Canova.[37] Cobb initially "urged Carothers Washington trip so that you [Bryan] could have full report from him of situation and full understanding with him for the future" with regard to conduct and information on which to base presidential policy.[38] The next week Cobb clarified additional allegations from G. R. Hackley, Southern Pacific's commercial agent in Mexico, against Carothers and made yet another defense of Carothers.[39]

While Carothers's fate hung in the balance, Cobb greeted a new presidential fact-finding agent, Paul Fuller, on August 12, and assisted him in locating and interviewing Villa. Fuller, directed by Bryan to Cobb,

> found Mr. Cobb very vigilant on the subject of Mexico and informed about all the rumors as well as facts. His impressions, gathered from the many sources available in El Paso, which is the headquarters or refuge of partisans of Huerta and of Carranza and of Villa, as well as of the birds of prey who hope to profit by the distressing situation, only confirmed those I had already gathered in New York and Washington as to the mercenary character of a number of the men in the immediate service of the two leaders.[40]

Cobb misinterpreted Fuller's mission of fact-finding when, on Fuller's departure, he urged Washington "that it would be well to keep Mr. Fuller with Villa and Carranza alternately until they come to an agreement, and until each of them really understands and appreciates administration's policy."[41] That Bryan subsequently acted on Cobb's suggestion to have Fuller contact Alvaro Obregón, Constitutionalist general and later president of Mexico, in Mexico City demonstrated Cobb's quick ability to adjust to and subtly influence events.[42] As Fuller departed, the real challenge and opportunity materialized.

An opportunity to ease Villa-Carranza tensions and influence events appeared with the projected visit of Villa and Carrancista General Alvaro Obregón to El Paso on their way to jointly resolve disputes in Sonora.[43] Cobb acted independently as Carothers, returned to duty, initially remained in Mexico. Bryan granted Cobb overall authority including having "the army officers report to you and receive instructions from you in the matter."[44] Despite his authority and position Cobb allowed the situation to "drift."[45] Cobb acquiesced to a proposal of Villa's officers for U.S. and Mexican generals to meet rather than object to Villa's "keen desires" and create "irreparable injury" or "abuse [his] authority by antagonizing the military here."[46] Coincidentally, Bryan's message with Cobb's authority arrived as General John J. Pershing sat with Cobb in the collector's office discussing the situation.[47] Cobb retained his composure and regained control when he prevented Villa from meeting Pershing on the bridge between Juárez and El Paso without Obregón or other Constitutionalist representatives. Cobb escorted the entire Mexican entourage of Villistas and Carrancistas to the bridge personally and additionally "vetoed every suggestion of a banquet or any other function where there might be indiscreet talk."[48]

Villa and Obregón departed El Paso for Nogales, Arizona, on August 27 with a detachment of soldiers as escort. Carothers followed a day behind in a chase train. To prevent any embarrassment of a hitherto successful situation, Cobb and Carothers recommended that the return trip not include El Paso and that the army remain aloof from a return courtesy call.[49] Before Pershing received orders reflecting the latter recommendation, Cobb, returning to a policy of drift, recommended a return via El Paso, a return call from General Pershing, and, if results in Sonora warranted, a commendation for Villa and Obregón.[50] Cobb's motivation centered on a belief "that there is an opportunity to divert the mind and ambition of Villa from military pursuits to peace endeavors, provided he receives equal commendation and fame."[51] Bryan immediately responded with short notes of commendation for both Mexican generals which were presented on September 1 during Pershing's return call.[52] Cobb earned no direct accolades for his efforts, but he must have experienced a sense of satisfaction at the results of his most severe test at the end of a challenging month. Obregón won Cobb's favor in the episode as he favorably impressed Cobb as "sincere in his peace efforts and tactful in his actions."[53]

Cobb's next diplomatic action involved little grandeur, even less success, and serves to illustrate his junior status. On January 27, 1915, Bryan asked Cobb to prevent a prize fight in Juárez, in response to an El Paso minister's plea. After looking into the matter, Carothers and Cobb proved unequal to the task. Nonetheless, the fight did not occur. Promoters' financial considerations changed the venue to Havana, Cuba.[54]

Throughout 1914 and into early 1915, Cobb provided an increasing number of reports on incidents, temporary situations, and trends within Mexico and the revolution. In addition to the information provided, they demonstrated a growing appreciation of rudimentary intelligence procedures. Cobb's first foundation for his information came from the multitude of people whom he knew personally and his own customs force. As an aspiring and ambitious politician, he had many contacts. As he related to General Scott, "I have come in contact with Mexicans, in politics, for over thirteen years, but very frequently realize that even yet I am not on to all their curves" and "I mix and mingle with people of all factions, with a view to keeping informed."[55] Skepticism of his sources would play its role also. Another element in his growing ability came from contacts within the army's nascent intelligence community.

If Cobb's first steps in diplomacy were tentative, his first efforts in intelligence were even more so. From February until October 1915, Lazaro De La Garza, who acted as Villa's agent in Ciudad Juárez, served as Cobb's most frequently exploited source. Either in ignorance or to tout his contacts, Cobb initially exercised little effort in concealing this or other sources. De La Garza provided information on Villa's political operations, including information on disputes between Villa and Carranza, Villa's personal movement and personal assignments, and insights into Villa's financial dealings.[56] In return, De La Garza attempted, and failed, to obtain unofficial support for Villa from Cobb.[57] In addition to De La Garza, Cobb also gained information from other Villa officials who remained more anonymous. Most importantly from these sources and "from two of my friends who are associated with General Villa and may be accepted by you as reliable information," he obtained background on General Eulalio Gutiérrez, the newly appointed temporary president of the Convention of Aguascalientes, which was an attempt at a provisional revolutionary government.[58]

A caricature of Cobb titled "ZACH WAS BUSY" from a portfolio of portraits in the local paper depicting activity during the American Mining Convention of 1905. Cobb had lured the convention to the El Paso area the previous year. The rendition also captures Cobb's energy and activity reported by others. El Paso Herald, *November 15, 1905, page 5.*

In conjunction with his reports on political conditions in El Paso relevant to the situation in Mexico, Cobb provided data on ammunition legally moving into Mexico and other information of military interest. As early as August 1914, in his first report the State Department forwarded to the general staff, Cobb provided "authentic information," possibly from De La Garza, of Villa's numbers and dispositions.[59] His interest in military information may in part reflect contacts with U.S. Army intelligence. In April 1914 Cobb had a working relationship with Capt. Harry Cootes of the U.S. 13th Cavalry. During the crisis atmosphere of that month, which the landing at Veracruz had created, Cobb had volunteered to raise and command a "volunteer regiment of border cavalry" and serve with his friend, Captain Cootes.[60] Captain Cootes, in a letter of May 17, 1914, mentioned Cobb to their mutual friend, General Scott, formerly military commander in El Paso and now assistant chief of staff of the army in Washington. Cootes also noted the following:

> We need some money badly here for use in secret service and Genl P [Pershing] told me that he had received a letter from you stating that you would help us out—I am almost ashamed to ask the help of some of those who have given us their time and men free for all these past months.[61]

Contacts with the army regarding intelligence matters included an introduction of De La Garza to General Pershing in May.[62] In June 1915 Cobb shared information with the Fort Bliss provost marshal used in a report to General Pershing regarding garrison conditions in Juárez.

> Mr. Cobb's agent in Juárez reported to me that the strength of the garrison was then about five hundred but that they changed them very frequently to keep the soldier from becoming restless and that the strength of the garrison was very changeable.[63]

Despite this outline of coordination, Cobb did not always enjoy a close working relationship with military commanders.

As the collector of customs, Cobb exercised primary responsibility for enforcement of the arms embargo against Mexico. In July 1914 Brigadier General Tasker Bliss, commander of the U.S. Army Southern Department at San Antonio, Texas, which included Fort Bliss and El Paso, complained to General Scott of the performance of customs in El Paso.

> From all the information I can get the Customs officials make perfunctory examination (even if they make any at all) of such things as *coal cars, oil tanks, dynamite boxes* (exported by permission of the State Department), etc., etc. The Army cannot interfere with articles that are nominally in the jurisdiction of the

Customs Department.. . . . I think that the Treasury department ought to issue the most stringent orders to its Inspectors and Customs officials generally and take steps to see that they are enforced. (Emphasis added.) [64]

Bliss also sent similar messages to the secretary of war who forwarded copies to the Treasury and State departments.[65] Bliss had a few days earlier issued confidential orders to Pershing to inspect cars crossing the border and assist the collector of customs. In response to his directions, Pershing reported to Bliss on July 20:

The other day upon receipt of your telegram, to consult the collector of customs regarding his examination of oil cars, I sent an officer with it to Mr. Cobb, and latter said his men examined every car, but that evening I saw Captain Bash, 16th Infantry, at the Paso del Norte Hotel, and he said they did not examine them at all. Mr. Cobb was in the hotel at the time, so I went to him and told him what Captain Bash had just told me. He said he had given positive orders, but would see that they were obeyed and would cooperate with us. Every effort will therefore now be made to detect shipments if there are any.[66]

This activity resulted in Treasury orders to Cobb on July 22, 1914, to thoroughly inspect "all coal cars, oil tanks and dynamite boxes passing through El Paso, Texas, into Mexico to prevent smuggling of arms and munitions of war."[67] By the beginning of August, both the army and customs complained to Washington of their inability to halt the smuggling of munitions.[68]

From the aftermath of this embarrassment and other lesser problems of coordination with federal agencies in El Paso, Cobb learned an important lesson: execution of responsibilities in the volatile circumstance of the border area required cross-departmental cooperation. In April 1915 Cobb took action on this lesson. He hosted a dinner at the El Paso del Norte "for representatives of the various government departments in the city."[69] Notable among the over thirty attendees stand General Pershing, Lt. James Lawton Collins (later chief of staff, U.S. Army), Clifford Beckham of the Bureau of Investigation, U.S. consul in Juárez T. D. Edwards, S. E. Boovee of the Secret Service, George J. Harris of Immigration, and U.S. district clerk and part-time cryptologist George B. Oliver. Cobb would reap benefits in the near future from this attempt at federal coordination.

In addition to providing reports of events, Cobb also submitted commentary and suggestions to Washington. From this material an indication of his attitude toward the principal actor across the border in Mexico emerges. Cobb's primary concern with Villa involved the growing influence of special interests and Villa's confiscation of private property. As early as July 1914 Cobb saw Villa's freedom from "big special interests" as an important point in the general's favor with which Bryan agreed.[70] A month later Cobb expressed concern that "through concessions to associates Villa is surrounded by corruption [and] is in danger of being drawn into an alliance with big special interests. In my opinion situation is extremely dangerous."[71] Villa's seizure of property brought forth initially mild but increasingly negative comments. In Cobb's opinion, profits of $500,000 from 35,000 unbranded cattle threatened the peace during July. By September, Cobb noted the "worst feature connected with Villa is the fact that he is surrounded by men who seek graft through his favor. I am afraid that this condition may present the greatest difficulties of the future."[72] Bryan recognized Cobb's concerns.[73] Cobb did not return to the theme of confiscated property until March 1915. In his strongest statement to date, he repudiated Villa's confiscation of property and urged "that respect and protection for American and foreign property-owner is an equal right to all bona fide foreign property owners as distinguished from special favors."[74] He further suggested linking Villa's attitude toward property with possible recognition. During the next two months, Cobb heartened as Carothers, whom he influenced on the importance of this issue, reported progress toward respect for property rights.[75]

These opinions and concerns do not create an image of Cobb as an enthusiastic supporter of Villa. Neither do they convey an

impression of Cobb as vehemently anti-Villista at this time. Of
Cobb's contemporaries, Letcher found him a Villa partisan and
another anonymously mailed a spent bullet, "Para los gringos villistas [*sic*]."[76] During this period, Cobb saw Villa at worst as "a bubble,
that is terribly strained. A serious reverse would probably be followed by a general collapse."[77] Or that Villa would "make a grand-
stand play against the United States intending to boost himself."[78]

Cobb's view of Villa assumes importance because historians have
accused the collector of taking and voicing vehemently anti-Villa
stands during this period. Predominately, these positions center on
Cobb's refusal to export coal to Villa during his aborted 1914 drive to
Mexico City.[79] The record fails to support allegations of Cobb or
U.S. Customs denying Villa coal. As noted previously, General Bliss
complained of customs not inspecting coal cars crossing the border
and caused the issuance of such orders to Cobb in July. The previous
month Carothers reported "that C. [Carranza] prevents Villa getting
coal; that because C. keeps all rolling stock Villa sends to Monterey
District."[80] Later in June Cobb reported, "General Villa had
intended pushing south from Zacatecas, but has changed plan with
approval of all Generals. Will return north and distribute army from
Torreón to Juárez, leaving Zacatecas to Natera. Changed plan following reasons: . . . second, refusal of Carranza to furnish coal."[81] A
settlement between Carranza and Villa, which Carothers apparently
brokered, permitted a Villa agent to "control railroads and coal
fields."[82] On August 1, 1914, Cobb reported that Villa "is buying and
shipping coal."[83] Finally, considering Villa's violent reputation, one
can hardly imagine that he would endure an anti-Villista Cobb prior
to his meeting with Pershing and Obregón during the Sonoran
crisis.[84] Reports of Cobb preventing the shipment of coal to Villa in
conjunction with Carranza forces appear unfounded.

In late 1914 and early 1915, Cobb's paltry intelligence reporting
declined as the local scene quieted. Between Carothers's and
Canova's increasing number of messages from the Aguascalientes
Convention, Cobb paid a visit in December to Washington to attend
to customs business.[85] From administration of telegrams to and from

Aguascalientes and Washington and in light of administrative complaints and comments from the code room in Washington during this period, Cobb perfected his use of the State Department's Red Code.[86] Proper use of codes represents an important trait for any intelligence agent. Cobb, after initially utilizing Carothers's code book, had received his own in May 1914 and, failing to obtain a replacement and reflecting its use, had his copy rebound in January 1915 for $3.50.[87] Typically, a coded message would appear as follows:

> Very confidential fakpi lawrence kidding millest dearing professes
> blair trumpet scratcher offertory autocratic unprofessed exprobra-
> tion obstruct autocratic goram newberry cliff flimsy. COBB"

Decoded, this means:

> Lazaro de la Garza informs me confidentially quote Villa is
> very short of ammunition. Unquote Endeavoring obtain ammu-
> nition from New York by express. COBB[88]

After mastering code and on returning from Washington, Cobb's reporting for the first half of 1915 concentrated on local events. Increasingly, a counterrevolutionary group centered on former Mexican President Victoriano Huerta and Mexican general of revolutionary fame, Pascual Orozco, gained strength in El Paso and Mexico. Cobb linked the depreciation of Villa's currency with that movement. On April 15, 1915, he reported:

> The currency problem is as near to hopeless as anything can be.
> They ship through here and grind out quantities of it, although
> the supply already exceeds the demand. It appears inevitable
> that Villa's currency will continue to go down. This, so far as
> can be seen from here, applies to the Carranza currency also.[89]

The following month Cobb would report increased financial and military support for Huerta's forces.[90] In early June 1915, Cobb observed:

With the indications of Villa's economic distress, the counter-revolutionists are very active again. Orozco is in town, there are many indications that they are preparing to act. . . . I am of the opinion that some officers in the Juárez garrison are in league with Orozco, that there is a decided possibility that Orozco might take Juárez any night, discontent masses would receive him cordially, and that much of Villas [*sic*] army might turn to him especially those commanded by ex-federals.[91]

Cobb reported the buildup of counterrevolutionary forces in El Paso from multiple sources such as a banker close to local and New York financial figures, public officials, the postmaster at Fabens, Texas, and newspapers, particularly the *El Paso Times*.[92] Showing some discretion and awareness of his potential significance, Cobb used these intermediaries to stay away from direct involvement with and collection from the plotters in order not to create an appearance of support.[93] Additionally, he took discreet steps to discourage any appearance of support when he urged Washington not to release Rodrigo Quevedo, a Huerta supporter jailed at Fort Bliss. As an indicator of his influence, based on Cobb's single message, the Department of State took quick and continuing action to comply.[94]

June 1915 found Cobb with an extensive and growing machine. Exposure to the functions of intelligence had opened new paths to influence and opportunities for service. Several basic fundamentals of intelligence work were mastered. Additionally, he had established contacts with several of the Mexican factions. Ranking officers of the United States government in El Paso worked with increasing coordination under Cobb's guidance. Despite his accomplishments as an intelligence operative, Cobb still stood as an enthusiast. However, over time and with limited direction, Cobb's professionalization would provide a diverse, reliable, and continuing source of intelligence information on military, economic, and diplomatic events. The unexpected challenges of late June would find Cobb prepared and allow him to move with speed and determination. Increasingly, he would act independently of Carothers.

Two Leaders:
Arrest and
Defeat

JUNE 1915 PROVED A PIVOTAL MONTH for Cobb. Villa and Obregón had met in a series of fierce battles contesting the fate of the revolution around the town of Celaya, north of Mexico City, in April, at León through May, and at Aguascalientes during July.[1] Ramifications from Villa's defeats at Celaya (April 6–7 and 13–15) became increasingly clear by June. Significant among these stood, as a result of Villa's dwindling financial resources and territory, confiscation of property which supported greed, not revolutionary requirements, and threatened not only chaos but famine within Villa's territory. While Carothers maintained some influence with the erratic revolutionary leader, Cobb's marginal support for both men dwindled. Counterrevolutionary forces in El Paso and Mexico, moving with increased boldness, demanded a response but their suppression seemed a still frustrating and futile goal. President Wilson provided, at least in Cobb's view, a policy regarding Mexico around which action could center. The president's June 2 proclamation promised the following:

active moral support to some man or group of men, if such may
be found, who can rally the suffering people of Mexico to their
support in an effort to ignore, if they can not unite, the warring
factions of the country, return to the constitution of the Republic
so long in abeyance, and set up a government in Mexico City
which the great powers of the world can recognize and deal
with, a government with whom the program of revolution will
be a business not merely a platform.[2]

In this statement, Cobb found hope and a promise of plans for
future actions. He would find himself in the confusion of factions
and opinions circling the border, a focal point for action in support
of the administration's real and imagined plans for Mexico.

Whatever its various interpretations, Wilson's policy clearly supported constitutional procedures and revolutionary, not counterrevolutionary, forces.[3] For both Mexican and U.S. officials, a primary figure of concern among the plotters against the revolution was
Victoriano Huerta. The exiled former president of Mexico had
arrived in New York from Spain in April 1915 with the financial
backing of German intelligence agents.[4] Huerta left New York on
June 24, ostensibly to visit San Francisco. In Chicago, however, he
went south to Kansas City and, on the night of June 25, boarded a
train for El Paso. Rumors denying and affirming Huerta's arrival
fueled speculation in the El Paso press and counsel to "Take a choice
and wait."[5] Despite open public speculation and uncertainty, Cobb
telegraphed a report to the State Department at one in the afternoon.

Associated Press correspondent advises me of private information that Huerta left Kansas City last night on Rock Island. His
train reaches El Paso Sunday morning six thirty.[6]

Less than four hours after its receipt in Washington, Cobb
received instructions from newly appointed Secretary of State
Robert Lansing to "Advise immediately and cooperate with El
Paso representative Department of Justice."[7] Events in El Paso
had already passed such general instructions.

Cobb learned from railroad sources, perhaps the same ones used in an *El Paso Morning Times* article on Sunday, June 27, that Huerta intended "to leave train in Newman Station, twenty miles north of El Paso."[8] Probably at Cobb's urgings, a reception committee formed and proceeded to meet the train. The party consisted of Special Agent Beckham of the Bureau of Investigation, Deputy United States Marshals Jere deBose and Edward Bryant, a detachment of cavalry and two of infantry totaling 25 men under the command of Colonel George H. Morgan of the 15th Cavalry, several newspapermen, and Cobb. Arriving at sunrise, the caravan of eight automobiles found Pascual Orozco "behind some shrubbery near the railroad" which confirmed their surmise of possible unneutral activity.[9] Some of the soldiers quickly formed a perimeter around the site. According to the *Herald* report a period of confusion then ensued.

> It was discovered, suddenly, that Newman is in the state of New Mexico and its station is but a hundred yards from the Texas boundary line. Realizing that they could make no arrests in the state of New Mexico, a telegram was immediately sent to the train dispatcher in El Paso to issue orders that train No. 1 be instructed not to stop until it was clearly within the state of Texas. Soldiers were placed up and down the tracks and a red flag was procured with which to flag the train in case it attempted to go by.[10]

Ready or not, at 6:35 a.m. the train rolled in and stopped in Texas. Colonel Morgan, Special Agent Beckham, and Cobb boarded the train and found Huerta in his compartment. Offered a choice between western hospitality and protection as their guest or arrest based on warrants, Huerta chose to accompany his host, Cobb, freely.

Alighting from the train, Huerta greeted Orozco, who also accepted the invitation. Huerta, Orozco, Colonel Morgan, and Cobb sat in one of the cars and the convoy proceeded to Cobb's office in the Federal Building.[11] En route, Huerta stopped at the

El Paso Country Club for refreshments and then visited his daughter, identified only as Mrs. Fuentes, and her husband at the Georgette apartments. In Cobb's office, while awaiting instructions from Washington, Huerta graciously accepted a gift of cigarettes from Cobb, examined "a home-made shell produced by the Villa factories for the use of their cannon," and engaged in friendly combat with the assembled reporters.[12] Charged with conspiracy to violate U.S. neutrality laws and inciting an armed revolt in a friendly country, Huerta and Orozco became prisoners. Fearing a potentially violent demonstration, Mayor Tom Lea of El Paso requested transfer of the two prisoners to Fort Bliss.

Such fears and the minor public demonstrations following the arrest illustrate the growing cultural and political divisions within the El Paso community. Cobb approved of the plan, possibly reflecting his knowledge of a recent Orozco-Lea meeting or Lea's status as a nonmachine politician.[13] En route, the car transporting them caught fire, but on their safe arrival they faced arraignment before United States Commissioner George B. Oliver in the post administration building. Pleading not guilty, the accused had their bail set at a reduced level of $15,000 for Huerta and $7,500 for Orozco at the suggestion of Mayor Lea. Following posting of bail from local supporters, Orozco went to his house and Huerta to the home of his daughter, both under the observation of federal officers.

Cobb received local and national credit for the arrests. El Paso newspapers, particularly the *El Paso Herald,* noted Cobb's prominent role.

Cobb Says He Stopped Revolt

That the detention of Gen. Huerta and Gen. Orozco early Sunday morning "nipped another Mexican revolution," is the expressed belief of Zack [sic] Lamar Cobb, collector of customs, who caused the detention of the two men. Mr. Cobb had information that led him to believe that Huerta was to be taken by Orozco at once into Mexico to lead a military expedition possibly against Juárez.

Collector Cobb, who headed the delegation that met Gen. Huerta at Newman, N.M., Sunday morning and "invited" him to become the guest of the collector, said he acted first and reported to Washington afterwards.[14]

In addition to his previous communication with Washington, denied above, Cobb did indeed report to Washington afterwards. While Huerta and Orozco sat in his office, Cobb wired Washington to note their presence in the Federal Building and in the process filled in some missing background on the incident.

> *Agent Beckham has received instructions to detain them. Prior to the receipt of these instructions, by reason of your June 26, 8 p.m. and urgency of situation, I insisted upon the course pursued and assumed responsibility therefore. . . .* We prepared warrants if necessary to use same, but found it unnecessary. Beckham invited Huerta and Orozco to accompany us to Federal Building without arrest, which they did. Without display we have treated them with consideration and every proper courtesy. Huerta is suave though Orozco is not suave. I am sure they had revolutionary plans and that the action here has been both right and timely. While I assume full responsibility for the course taken I respectfully suggest and recommend that both Colonel Morgan and Mr. Beckham should be commended by their respective Departments for the discretion shown by them. Beckham will make detailed report.[15] (Emphasis added.)

In addition to local recognition, kudos came to Cobb from Washington in two forms. In a short note from the acting secretary of state expressing appreciation for "prompt, efficient action," Cobb received his official recognition and thanks.[16] The second form of recognition, a more subtle accolade, came with Lansing's forwarding of Cobb's entire initial and subsequent reports to President Wilson.[17]

Before continuing Cobb's involvement with Huerta, some comments based on the record are in order. Apparently Cobb had no knowledge of any Huerta-German coordination available now to historians and in Washington at the time based on wiretaps placed on Huerta's hotel room.[18] Nor, based on the reported surprise at finding Orozco at Newman, did he have prior proof of a plan to move Huerta to Mexico. Cobb and Agent Beckham acted primarily on their own, bolstered with the minimal guidance Washington provided. Cobb's assumption of responsibility did not represent an idle statement but recognition of his role as the principal motivator in the events and acceptance of possible condemnation from Washington. He had acted without the support of his benefactor Bryan or the local support of Carothers. Emboldened with his independence and success, based principally on private information, even if quickly made public, Cobb would increasingly act with independence and boldness in pursuit of his understanding of State Department goals.

Even after the arrest and accolades, Cobb's role in the incident continued. He urged the careful treatment of Huerta to avoid offending Mexican sentiments and pointed out the continuing threat counterrevolutionary forces posed in El Paso.[19] Cobb believed this threat increased with the mayor acting as Huerta's attorney, which "necessarily will affect the attitude of the El Paso authorities," because of business "sentiment here strongly with Huerta," and he "can buy Juárez authorities whenever he is ready."[20] As demonstrations in support of Huerta continued and the legal system slowly moved forward, Cobb increasingly urged the removal of the two from the border.[21] Cobb's insight on Mexican internal conditions, particularly of a possible Villa collapse that he feared Huerta could exploit, included a nine-page "memorandum from Mr. O'Hea, the British Vice-Consul at Gómez Palacio, to his employer, Mr. Brittingham, a prominent American, interested in factories there."[22] Even with the escape of Orozco on July 3 and Huerta's second arrest and imprisonment in the city jail and then at Fort Bliss, Cobb received no State Department response to his urgent and repeated requests to move Huerta from the border. Not until July 9 would State advise Cobb that the Huerta matter resided with the Department of Justice.[23]

Following President Wilson's proclamation of June 2 and Cobb's handling of the Huerta visit to El Paso, another aspect of concern in Mexico—a conservative counterrevolutionary movement—had suffered a severe setback if not a death blow. This did little immediately to arrest the continuing chaos, disorder, and suffering in Mexico. Villa and Carranza responded to Wilson's proclamation on June 10 and 11 respectively. Neither unconditionally committed to its support.[24] Additionally, Mexico City continued to suffer factional turnovers, looting, rape, murder, and the threat of starvation. Constitutionalist forces violated the January 1915 status quo agreement, seizing Naco and threatening Nogales in Sonora. Most importantly, along the border came ripples from the bizarre Plan of San Diego in the lower Rio Grande Valley, "which called for nothing less than a Mexican-American rebellion and the establishment of an independent republic of the Southwest."[25] Finally, intrigues revolving around Americans and a variety of Mexican personalities grew bolder and more numerous.[26] Despite all these distractions, overall policy remained steadfast: "Support the revolution, avoid intervention, and attempt to influence the rebel leaders into the path of justice and moderation by means of diplomatic influence."[27]

Cobb, while maintaining an interest in assisting administration policy and frustrated with unsuccessful attempts to move Huerta from the border as a means of influence and participation, quickly shifted his attention to other issues of interest in the local area which he could impact. Graft, almost a form of government in Mexico at the time, incurred his particular wrath because it required implementation by rotten and selfish officials, endangered property rights, maintained Villa in power, and adversely impacted the populace. Assisting Red Cross representatives in Juárez, he pointed to "exhaustion of last year's crop, the shortage of this year's," and graft as the indicators of future starvation.[28] Both Villa and Huerta supporters earned strong condemnation. Hector Ramos, Villa's secret service and general agent in El Paso; Colonel Juan Medina, commanding in Gómez Palacio; and Villa's brother, Hipólito, surfaced frequently in reports of graft and deteriorating social, military, and economic conditions.[29] Believing that a plan existed in Washington, Cobb frequently urged various courses of action for consideration.[30] His most important function over the next several months became that of chronicler and assistant to Villa's demise.

Two themes dominated Cobb's concerns and reports from July through October of 1915: Villa's deteriorating status and the need to take action to remove him. The defeat of Villa at León on June 7, and Obregón's capture of Aguascalientes on July 10, 1915, clearly indicated to Cobb not only Villa's growing military weakness but also a point of economic significance.

> His [Villa's] expenses remain about the same, he having bought and received through Juárez over seven million cartridges since June first, while his sources of revenue are reduced as to territory and are constantly becoming less as to means. The Villa government and army cannot be legitimately sustained by his available resources.[31]

El Paso remained the financial and logistical linchpin of Villa's organization. Manifestations of Villa's growing weakness foreshadowed his imminent collapse, according to Cobb. Initially, this reinforced old fears of Huerta or other conservative forces suborning Villa's forces and further exacerbating the Mexican problem.[32] Time and the demise of Orozco in September 1915 and Huerta on January 10, 1916, eased these concerns. Anxiety continued, however, over confiscation of private, particularly foreign, property and its sale north of the border with the attendant continuation of Villa's forces and the threat of famine and suffering in Mexico.

Reflecting his apprehension, Cobb provided Washington frequent reminders of Villa's reprehensible actions and pending collapse. The seizure of the Brittingham's Jaborena Company in Torreón received strong attention as an example of Villa's methods. Cobb's pleas in this case resulted in Secretary Lansing's requesting General Scott to seek specific protection for the Jaborena Company along with other foreign interests during the Scott-Villa talks of August 1915 in El Paso.[33] Cobb, assuming the existence of a Washington plan to deal with Villa if not Mexico through the Argentina, Brazil, and Chile (ABC) conference convened in August 1915, continued to forward information regarding Villa's financial, political, and organizational collapse. Rather than hastening Villa's immediate downfall, Cobb's messages contributed to a scheme to support Villa temporarily.

Since at least November 1914, when Villa seized the Ciudad Juárez municipal slaughterhouse, Villa had received income from the sale of slaughtered beef. While the success of this operation endured several reverses, in July 1915 the United States Department of Agriculture (USDA) had "forced the closure of the Juárez plant."[34] Lansing, realizing Villa's desperate condition (in large part from Cobb's reports), and desiring to maintain Villa as a viable alternative to the intractable Carranza during the ABC conference, "wanted to relax restrictions on the shipment of cattle from Mexico to the United States."[35] Reaction came swiftly.

> Proposed reopening of the Juárez plant engendered opposition from United States cattlemen as well as from Zack [sic] Cobb. Cobb formally protested the packinghouse reopening, arguing that cattlemen in Mexico were forced to use Villa as their agent or else suffer confiscation of their entire herds.[36]

Cobb clearly did not understand the nature of planning exercised in Washington. An equally strong and surprised reaction, according to Larry D. Hill, came from President Wilson.

> At first the president was puzzled, unable to understand why Lansing would want to bolster Villa and prolong the conflict in Mexico. When the secretary explained his purposes, Wilson agreed that Villa should be allowed to export beef.[37]

Despite objections, wonderment, and finally reopening of the slaughterhouse, Villa's decline continued and his situation only worsened when on October 19, the United States extended *de facto* recognition to Carranza.[38] Official policies supporting recognition of Carranza and Cobb's role in their development and execution would strain his relationship with Washington and his official authority to the breaking point.

Ignoring perceptions of confusion in Washington, in late October 1915 Cobb perceived opportunity in the chaos of Mexico. Villa, compressed into the state of Chihuahua, desperately tried to expand his territory and border base with an expedition into neighboring Sonora where he ultimately "lost his capacity for responsible leadership."[39] This operation reached an earlier climax with Villa's defeat at Agua Prieta, Sonora, across from Douglas, Arizona. Carranza forces had reinforced Agua Prieta with troops transported through Eagle Pass, Texas, across New Mexico and into Arizona. Villa's absence from Chihuahua weakened the loyalty of his remaining supporters and further emphasized his dependence on the slender thread of Juárez–El Paso as a source of funds and material. Continued sale and taxation of exported goods remained crucial to Villa's financial health. Essential to this effort, and any long-range military mobility in Chihuahua, stood the railroad.[40]

Cobb, anticipating recognition of Carranza, which occurred on October 19, reported on October 16 that while Villa continued to disintegrate gradually, the "chief element of Villa cohesion is his commercial organization at El Paso and Juárez. The profits come from property stolen in Mexico and marketed through El Paso."[41] Closing the Port of El Paso provided a means of ending Villa's depredations. Cobb recognized this as "a critical time on the border and not only for present results but as well for future effects."[42] Naturally, federal authorities in El Paso cooperated, Cobb reported, to "carry out wishes of Washington as expressed in instructions received, and with simultaneous effort not to exceed instructions."[43] Future events would make this a prophetic statement for Cobb. Following instructions primarily meant delaying shipments for forty-eight hours.[44] But this stopgap measure had little real effect and on October 27, Cobb again urged strong action.

The way to avoid a crisis at Agua Prieta, the way to remove any Villa influence in the Brownsville situation [a reference to the Plan of San Diego], and the way to turn the State of Chihuahua to Carranza is to lock this port up so tight that these grafters cannot operate. . . . *By closing this port we can get the sympathy and cooperation of practically everybody,* by allowing the grafters to continue to operate we will get the opposition of important influences.[45] (Emphasis added at the State Department in the original.)

Coupled with an October 22 suggestion from Cobb to embargo coke and coal, State took action.[46] Unlike a year earlier, Villa was cut off from the coal fields of Coahuila and depended solely on the importation of coal and coke from El Paso.

Based on Cobb's telegram, the State Department's Division of Mexican Affairs drafted letters to the secretary of the treasury for the president's signature. These drafts directed, among other actions, "the collector hereafter not to allow the exportation of coal and coke via El Paso."[47] While State's own solicitor questioned the suggestion's legality, thereby holding the proposal at State, letters in a similar vein went to the USDA and directly to Treasury.[48] Meanwhile, in response to an information copy from Cobb of one of his October 22 messages to State, Treasury directly informed Cobb:

Under opinion Attorney General Treasury decision thirty two three forty two coal and coke cannot be treated as munitions war. Your recommendation cannot therefore be approved. You should submit such questions to this Department instead of to State Department.[49]

In the midst of this bureaucratic activity in Washington resulting from his telegrams, Cobb received notice that State had requested USDA to cooperate with customs to detain "undesirable importations from Villa territory" and that State, after Cobb's objection to Treasury's initial response, acted "to have railroads cooperate with you to delay as much as possible coal and coke shipment via El Paso."[50] Given little authority and faced with interdepartmental bickering in Washington, Cobb nonetheless acted forcefully in conjunction with new allies.

Carranza's consul in El Paso, Andrés García, on October 27 "obtained state court injunction restraining railroads from returning Mexican railroad equipment to Juárez."[51] Enforcement would require a one-hundred-thousand-dollar bond and necessary funds were not locally available. In the meantime, pending arrival of funds and at Cobb's suggestion, letters from the Carranza consul to railroad officials provided a stopgap measure.[52] Cobb further assisted the effort with a reduction of the bond to five thousand dollars, permitting enforcement to begin on October 28.[53] Cobb gleefully reported to Washington that "no coal has gone over."[54] Beyond the immediate requirement, and coupled with a plea to Washington for support when local elements applied pressure, Cobb reported his motivation as follows:

> The one prevailing talk among our Americans in Mexico has been the demand for a strong hand. A strong hand here, provided most discreetly exercised, can do nothing but good.[55]

Cobb certainly seemed to fit the description, or at least wanted to.

In further proof of his discretion and to hasten resolution of the situation, Cobb also recommended a rather bizarre stratagem. In conjunction with the quiet movement of Carranza forces through the United States to engage Villa in Sonora, he advised authorities in Washington to:

> permit Carranza to disembark troops, bound from Eagle Pass to Douglas, at the Mexico–New Mexico line just across the river from El Paso. March three miles and surround Juárez, providing expressly that it must only be a siege with no firing upon either Juárez or El Paso. As soon as the seige [sic] was accomplished and telegraph and railroad lines taken there would be a general turn over [of Juárez and Chihuahua to Carranza].[56]

Fortunately, this message was marked "Personal," and despite a copy sent to the General Staff, remained that way.

Unfortunately, on November 1 the state court injunction barring the railroads from returning equipment dissolved. Only the railroads' cooperation and "such course as this office [collector of customs] may take" would prevent the export of coal essential to Villa.[57] For the next several weeks, Cobb, implicit in the record, pushed his authority and influence to the limit to achieve that goal. As Villa personally commanded his forces in Sonora, the collector pleaded with Washington for additional authority, played one department off against another, cajoled mining executives for cooperation, and simply refused to permit coal to move across the border. Additionally, with one exception, he used similar tactics to prevent the importation of livestock from Mexico. Cobb's single-mindedness and dedication as he worked towards Villa's collapse represented an impressive personal, although not a very professional, record.

Embargo of coal remained Cobb's primary weapon. While management of mining companies in New York demanded exportation of coal to keep mines open and smelters operating, Cobb

> told local representatives of their right to same, urging that Villa would take it probably, and appealing to them to help protect the property of Americans who had come out upon the call of our Government. It was agreed to let the coal remain here provided they could blame me to New York and that same could move whenever Villa got his, this all being confidential.[58]

Through tactics of patriotism, self-victimization, appeals to the common good, lack of favoritism, and probably some unreported veiled threats, all except one of the mining companies agreed not to export coal. Alvarado Mining Company under the management of A. J. McQuatters continued to push for coal.[59] With McQuatters in Washington to complain about the injunction, Cobb requested State to: "If consistent and possible please have him persuaded to telegraph El Paso agents not to insist on exportation."[60]

Aerial view of downtown El Paso and San Jacinto Plaza circa 1910 looking
generally southwest. The office of the collector of customs was located in the
four-story and towered Federal Building on the south side of the square
(the picture's left center). Mexico is in the background with Juárez to the left.
The railroad tracks are visible in the foreground (note the switching tower).
(Courtesy of the University of Texas at El Paso Library, Special Collections.)

State did not reply. Meanwhile, McQuatters's local agent complained to Treasury of Cobb's intransigence and Cobb reported to
Treasury, with "Personal" copies to State, that the Alvarado Mining Company acted as the only holdout among the local mining
companies and seemed strongly Villista.[61] Although forced under
Treasury oversight to release the coal, railroads "stopped and
refused exportation . . . upon order of higher officials [who] will
not permit exportation Villa coal."[62] The following day, Cobb
informed State, probably in an effort to gain its support against
Treasury, of further Treasury instructions.

There is absolutely no legal authority for Customs to interfere with any shipments to Mexico in usual course of commerce other than munitions of war. The Department insists upon you being governed accordingly and giving no more cause for complaints of this character.[63]

Specific sources of Cobb's support from the railroads remain unclear, although the injunction, letters to the railroads from the Carranza consul, and tactics similar to those used on the local mining companies possibly played a role. From information the Mexico Northwestern Railroad superintendent provided, Cobb could justify his previous action and report:

[M]ilitary train ready Juárez tomorrow as soon as coal is received. Therefore if Alvarado Company or any other coal goes to Juárez, it is practically certain it would be taken to use for this military purpose, which would endanger prospects of turnover garrison south of Juárez.[64]

Phelps Dodge Southwestern Railroad appeared ready to crumble to Villa pressure and deliver coal. Probably from his local legal contacts Cobb could report that "Attorney Phelps Dodge Company has advised Manager he must switch [railroad term] coal unless Government embargoes it, but at my request will delay same until tomorrow."[65] Additionally, Cobb also revealed some of his concerns, motivations, and feelings in a thinly veiled threat regarding consequences and a plea for support from State.

It is respectfully submitted that passage of this coal will be calamitous. I am representing absolutely the instructions of superiors, my November 10, 3P, and accordingly am unable to do anything to prevent this calamity. Those who abuse our Government in El Paso may be expected to abuse me in Washington. I am endeavoring to be so discreet as not to furnish material for abuse. The passage of this coal constitutes a peril, for the renewal of commerce that will pay Villa revenue, and for reviving of Villa spirit through[out] Chihuahua.[66]

This coal would not go to Mexico, as Washington received notification three hours later, along with some insight into Cobb's methods and sources, that: "We are greatly indebted to Johnson of Phelps Dodge, Southwestern Railroad; he found purchaser and acquired coal from parties demanding export from Villa. This apparently saves us again."[67]

Washington had provided mixed signs of support. Treasury maintained a hostile and legalistic attitude toward the unofficial embargo. State, in whose behalf Cobb envisioned his efforts as furthering some unknown plan, had indicated modest support, as previously noted, with promises of possible railroad and USDA cooperation. In light of continuous direct and indirect pleas for assistance from Washington, and before his local challenges and success became clear, Cobb discovered the isolation of a man of action. On November 11, Lansing notified Cobb of State's position.

> Your telegrams of November nine and ten regarding coal for Alvarado Company. It is feared that your anxiety to eliminate Villa element may cause friction between you and Treasury Department. You should comply with that Department's instructions. This Department cannot ask Treasury to countermand them. Department unable to locate McQuatters in Washington.[68]

Cobb responded the next day.

> Will restrict effort to seeking to furnish information and assure you there will be no friction with Treasury Department nor conflict with duties under respect for superiors of the Treasury Department.[69]

Coal flowed into Mexico, as did information into Washington, along with an estimated $300,000 in export taxes to Villa during the month of November.[70] Examination of this information flow during the remainder of 1915 provides some additional insight into Cobb's methods, concerns, and motivation.

First among Cobb's methods appears to be the use of a variety of sources. Earlier on November 11, 1915, details reached Washington of Villa's situation and intentions in Sonora based on a confidential report to Cobb from "Doctor J. W. Yard, citizen of El Paso of standing, who has been acting as surgeon in Villa army continuously for past fourteen months, and who left them at Naco last Sunday."[71] The Carranza consul in El Paso confidentially provided information on negotiations for the surrender of Villa commanders along the border and military developments in Chihuahua.[72] Observation of the arrivals in and departures from El Paso, probably by assistants since Cobb could not watch all the movements himself, furnished insights into mining company activities in Mexico.[73] Equally, friends and general passengers arriving in El Paso from Mexico volunteered observations on civil, military, and railroad conditions in Mexico.[74] Details on activities of Carranza and Villa forces along the border came from Cobb's own customs inspectors.[75] Reporters, as during the Huerta arrest, provided occasional information on Villa worthy of passing to Washington.[76] However, unknown but evaluated sources enabled Cobb to track Villa's personal movements and activities as well as the size of his force.[77] Obviously, the variety of sources provided a wide range of timely information on activities in Mexico.

These individual reports, when combined together, analyzed and submitted in a summary-type report, could provide a powerful tool to Washington. On December 9, 1915, largely from the sources above, Cobb submitted a piercing report of the situation in Mexico.[78] After commenting on the overall military situation, he noted that Carranza required more troops to properly secure his objectives. Also, Carranza needed to address the "church question [and] mining tax" to gain support in Chihuahua and north of the border. Following a review of Villa's financial situation, Cobb anticipated Villa, reduced in forces, would return to the border with increased viciousness and might bring "a crisis to the State of Chihuahua, such as may be reasonably feared, our Government will not only have to be strengthened here in the control of the privileges of this port, but will also have to have a military embargo."[79] Cobb closed with a note for Lansing.

> I am doing my best, and hope to be of service to him [Lansing] here; all the while wishing that Villa agents and agencies could be eliminated from the border, and also hoping and praying that Carranza may be wise enough to correct the economic and other underlying causes that furnish the sympathy, if not the actual support, to sustain opposition to the de facto government.[80]

Despite Washington's lack of support for what he must have viewed as an effective plan to rid northern Mexico of Villa and a partially fulfilled promise to limit himself to providing information, Cobb continued to press for action against Villa. Constitutionalist negotiations and military activities along the border had met with little success in spite of Villa's weakened condition after Agua Prieta. Cobb's first salvo in a renewed offensive for Washington's support came in a letter to Treasury on November 24, explaining local inability to enforce the embargo against munitions of war due to a dry Rio Grande. After outlining his inability and urging a military embargo, the letter closed with a plaintive observation: "We are cheerfully doing our best with an inadequate [customs] force, but do not like being in the position of rendering inefficient service, although it is beyond our power to make it efficient."[81] Cobb followed this with two telegrams to State outlining Villa's renewed boldness and continuing plunder.

> Situation here is reverting to that of two or three weeks ago. Carranza has, I believe, been double crossed by parties pretending to seek turnover of Juárez and probably participating in Juárez profits. . . . [C]ommercial forces of Villaism including especially traffic in Terrazas sheep and cattle, large revenue from Juárez gambling and racing and coinage and other disposition of metals stolen from mines and smelters, predominate in situation here.[82]

Having alerted and coordinated with both Treasury and State, a skillful bureaucratic move, Cobb exploited a new opportunity.

Acting in coordination with Department of Justice agents in late November, customs seized "several trucks [*sic*] of new Villa currency."[83] Cobb sought a definition of this material as a munition of war from Treasury. They declined the opportunity, although other federal agencies assumed jurisdiction under other statutes.[84] Frustrated in efforts to find new means to exert pressure on Villa, Cobb must have taken some satisfaction in the new coordination between Treasury and State, about which Under Secretary of the Treasury A. J. Peters informed Cobb.[85] Cobb had been "won once and for all" by Peters a year earlier as a result of his January 1915 support when Cobb "engaged in a struggle with a very powerful special interest, which struggle means more, perhaps, to me than anything I have ever undertaken."[86]

Minor advances in coordination with Washington had little real impact on the border, but a plan General Obregón proposed promised action and results. Carrancistas, frustrated in their negotiations and minor military efforts to seize Ciudad Juárez, "inquired to ascertain points between El Paso and Presidio opposite Ojinaga where Carranza troops might be crossed."[87] Cobb outlined the available crossing points east and west of El Paso to Lansing along with some legalities in a "CONFIDENTIAL—PERSONAL" telegram late on December 14.[88] Permission to cross at Fort Hancock came in a one-line message from Lansing the following day. Even as further details and implementing instructions moved to Washington and within the local area, the plan began to unravel. Local officials and citizens, including Sheriff Peyton Edwards, informed Cobb on December 17 of their objections to aspects of the proposal contained in their telegram to Texas Governor James E. Ferguson of December 15. While the Austin reply showed some confusion in associating current concerns with previous Mexican troop movements in support of operations in Douglas–Agua Prieta, Cobb, always the politician, advised caution to "maintain cordial relations with local officers and also to prevent aggrievance [*sic*]."[89] Concurring with local suggestions, Cobb proposed moving the crossing site "six miles west of El Paso in New Mexico and only four miles from Juárez."[90] Events in Juárez, however, rapidly overtook the intentions and accommodations of the moment.

Perhaps because of the threat of the plan, or because of continuing Carranza military movement toward the border or dwindling profits from loot, Villa officers in Juárez began serious negotiations to turn the city over.[91] Since at least October, predictions of turnover fell on Washington from Cobb. This goal had represented an immediate objective and measure of success in thwarting Villa's operations. Assurance of imminent turnover provided one promise which Cobb had used successfully with Treasury to extract additional delay in carrying out orders during the attempted coal embargo. Now, on December 18, Cobb reported renewed negotiations and urged State not to withdraw permission for the troop crossing as "fact such permission has been granted is the leverage controlling present strong tendency for Villa forces in Juárez and Chihuahua to turn over."[92] Cobb advised Washington of the progress made until December 20 when he reported agreement. Delays in implementation based on mutual mistrust and suspicion between the parties fueled Cobb's anxiety in reports to State. But the close of December witnessed Carranza's forces securing Juárez under Obregón's direction. The crisis and Villa seemed to have finally passed.

Carothers had long acted as Cobb's senior officer, but ties between the two men deteriorated with Villa's declining fortunes and then simply evaporated. While in July the two agents had shared sources of information, in August, as graft and looting rose in Villa's territory, Carothers defended Villa, causing Cobb to inform Washington that "Carothers is being lied to and imposed upon by false promises; his hopes of improving conditions are futile."[93] When Cobb submitted an unflattering description of Villa to Washington, interestingly, in an intercepted letter from José Santos Chocano, the "Peruvian Poet" with reported ties to President Estrada Cabera of Guatemala, Carothers found it "a vivid and correct description of the man [Villa] as he is at present."[94] Both men joined in demanding better security in Washington for their sources.[95] During Cobb's campaign to close the Port of El Paso, Carothers urged similar action in Naco and Nogales if Villa's Sonoran campaign succeeded.[96] In late November, Carothers described his relationship with Cobb to Washington as "delicate . . . even possibly to the extent of his criticizing my conduct to you."[97] Despite such apprehension, Cobb appears to have protected Carothers the following month when rumors of financial dealing between Carothers and Villa surfaced.[98] In the end, Carothers's loss of influence with a defunct Villa caused the former's fall from grace with both Cobb and Washington. Carothers had assisted Cobb in establishing influence and his utility had expired.[99]

As one relationship declined, another resurfaced with revitalized ties between Cobb and Obregón, originally initiated during the Villa-Obregón visit of August 1914. Immediately after the turnover, Cobb expressed "regrets through Consul García but have not deemed it wise to force an audience with General Obregón who is very much occupied until he expresses desire for same."[100] Consul García, as in the recent past, continued to act as a source of information for Cobb.[101] Cobb announced a change in sources with "General Obregón told me yesterday" and then reported details of Carranza troop movements and intentions to Washington."[102] In early January, Cobb crossed into Juárez with the Mexican consul and called on the officers there, possibly including General Obregón, and found them "far superior to type of officers who represented Villa."[103] Cobb also apparently participated in an El Paso Chamber of Commerce banquet for General Obregón, who crossed into Juárez from El Paso on December 31. Of the participants, Cobb observed:

> One of the chief speakers had been in my office ten days ago, with the sheriff, (my VALVI), agitating him to protest against permitting the Carranza troops from Sonora to come through

here, et cetera. . . . The fact that such people are now gushing over Obregón doesn't make that element of border Americans any less harmful in Mexican affairs. . . . Obregón is more intelligent than Villa. His actions here have, so far as I can see, been simple and in good sense. But, it is going to take the strongest qualities to hold him in line against the natural tendency for him to split off.[104]

Regarding Obregón, Cobb further advised:

This being the situation, I respectfully suggest the importance of our treating Obregón with respect, but also at the same time of letting him feel that the proper channel for international questions is through the State and Foreign Relations department of the respective governments.[105]

With Carothers waning and contact with Obregón rising, Cobb's future value seemed assured. Considering the opportunity for influence with the new regime, Cobb's obtuse suggestions for his own demise appear more than accidental.

In light of the improving conditions along the border with implementation of the long sought removal of Villa and Carranza's control of Juárez, opportunities for other changes seemed auspicious. On December 28, Cobb informed Lansing of his future intentions and a possible change in their relationship.

Upon the assumption that you wished it done, I have continued to forward Mexican information originating here. The desire to see the Mexican problem come out right, and to see the Administration enjoy that success, has been the motive and compensation for my efforts.

So long as I may be of any service, it is a pleasure. Whenever you wish my efforts modified, or should you at any time wish them discontinued, please let me know your desire. I have no false pride, nor any interest in Mexican affairs except as stated.[106]

Cobb, a few days later, reinforced images of his declining utility at the close of his letter covering the Obregón banquet and emphasizing formal state-to-state relations.

> With this thought in mind (my letter of the 28th instant), I am inclined to think that the occasion for my usefulness to you here is growing more limited, if not drawing to a close.[107]

In September, Lansing had requested that Cobb not attend a customs conference in New York "[i]n view of the critical situation now existing along the border."[108] Earlier, Lansing had acknowledged Cobb's "labor under extreme difficulties and for that reason your services are especially valuable."[109] On January 6, 1916, recognizing the changes since September, Lansing responded with diplomatic graciousness and evasiveness.

> I thank you for your letter of December 28th, and also for the clippings.
> I certainly appreciate your services, and the interest which you have taken in the Mexican situation, and hope that you will continue to manifest the same interest so long as may be necessary.[110]

An end of service to State seemed near indeed.

Cobb's performance had witnessed a tremendous horizontal and vertical growth. He had embraced the vague public policy of the president, "active moral support to some man or group of men," and turned it into meaningful action.[111] A counterrevolutionary cabal under Huerta and Orozco had been effectively disarmed. Both Carranza and Villa had seen the meaning of recognition not in the words from Washington but in the actions of an intelligence agent along the border. One man, acting in the light of local requirements, resolved a general policy and brought national power and influence to bear. Washington, while not intending the practice, had allowed the definition and implementation of policy in the field by an intelligence agent. While Cobb exerted a direct influence on events along the border, information would remain his primary and continuing means of gaining attention in Washington. He now provided a wide range of information from multiple sources, yet Washington provided little guidance to obtain this bounty. Generally his information proved accurate. When in doubt, he reported suspect information as rumors or with caveats regarding its reliability. From communications officer, he had grown into an agent of information. Circumstances would prove Lansing's tentative farewell premature, and Cobb's talents would find challenge in new and greater demands.

CHAPTER THREE

Chaos and Information Continue

DESPITE THE BEST HOPES and apparent intentions of Lansing and Cobb, the situation in Mexico, particularly in the state of Chihuahua, failed to improve with Villa's loss of Ciudad Juárez. In the course of the next year, conditions in Mexico settled into a malaise of graft, incessant but indecisive military action, and a struggle for survival, both at the factional level and, increasingly, at the individual noncombatant level. Despite optimistic expectation to the contrary, Villa proved far from inconsequential, Carranza demonstrated at best a marginal ability to establish a government in Chihuahua, and factional forces multiplied throughout 1916. Cobb continued to provide highly reliable information to the State Department, became a central authority for the department along the border and sustained his growth as an intelligence operative. His impact on events, marginalized with their complexity, and his decreased emotional involvement were reflected in a more detached reporting style.

Initially, Cobb presented Carranza's seizure of Juárez as promising a change for the better. Among his suggestions to Washington to exert a positive influence ranked restoration of consuls, who had been pulled from Mexico in late 1915.[1] Similar urgency attached to the removal of the munitions embargo.[2] Cobb's justifications for these recommendations illuminate his political philosophy and background.

> Their authorities [Mexican/Carrancista] must be brought to realize the responsibilities upon them—to know that they cannot create value in money without putting value behind money —and that the commerce essential to success cannot exist without security in the right of property. Realizing that human liberty is superior to property rights—Mexican affairs have taught me *that there comes a time when property rights constitute the essence of human liberty.*
>
> There is a way to cure this condition—short of military intervention—that is for the Americans to return to their property and for our Government to require the de facto government of Mexico—diplomatically, of course, but with unswerving firmness—that their American rights, so essential to the commerce of Mexico, be respected within the (legal) laws of Mexico.
>
> . . . Commerce is the solution for Mexico—short of military intervention.[3] (Emphasis made on file copy; internal paragraph spacing in original.)

Cobb, reflecting the depth of his opinions, requested forwarding of the letter to the president. State declined this suggestion but did respond positively, albeit slowly, to the suggestion to fill consular positions.[4]

Windows of opportunity for change creaked slowly shut. Cobb withdrew his previous recommendations on January 9, "following a foolish decree at Chihuahua [City] attempting to decree value into fiat money."[5] Concerns with an increasingly visible Carranza-Obregón split, as a harbinger of future problems, perhaps ranked in equal consideration.

As written you [State] on December 29th last, Obregón expected to have Chihuahua in his district and to maintain his headquarters there. Already this is changed and Chihuahua is placed in the district of [Carranza General Jacinto] Treviño. There is a political conflict between the Sonora element of Obregón and the Coahuila element that is more distinctly Carrancista. Chihuahua, lying between the two, has for the time been settled as stated.

There is probability that Obregón will be Secretary of War. This might be a wise arrangement.[6]

Cobb's rescinded suggestions more accurately reflected the challenge rather than the opportunity of events along the border. Additionally, strong reaction to such a seemingly trivial incident reflected his commitment to property rights and, in that context, responsible government.

Tensions, which had temporarily eased in December 1915, boiled with renewed vigor in El Paso. Unexpectedly, a Villista contingent stopped a train near Santa Ysabel, Chihuahua, on January 17, and executed 16 American mining engineers. As W. H. Timmons, a historian of the El Paso scene, reports:

With the arrival of the caskets, tensions in El Paso rose to the breaking point, resulting in fist fights, violence, and the city's first genuine race riot. . . . Although the police were able to prevent further attacks on Mexican-Americans, the atmosphere remained charged, a clear indication that if further trouble occurred, the city might explode again.[7]

Beyond the sensationalism involved, the executions meant that Americans could not safely return to their property. Correspondingly, commerce and the economy in Chihuahua would not rapidly resume. Cobb responded with a few messages of information to Washington clarifying the local and cross-border situation.[8] Meanwhile, another less spectacular incident seemed to have lit a short fuse.

The murder below Juárez of an American, Bert L. Akers, on January 21, and the lucky escape of his companion and eyewitness, Douglas Downs, created a local furor. Fortunately, Juárez officials quickly arrested, tried, and executed two suspects. Local press reports, carried nationally, doubted Mexican justice and, in questioning the identity and involvement of the executed, kept public passions inflamed. In the heightened situation, Cobb moved with surprising boldness to reduce "race feelings" on both sides of the border.[9] On January 23, with the permission of the Juárez commander, General Gabriel Gavira, Cobb accompanied Downs, U.S. District Attorney Crawford, and S. L. Pickney of the Bureau of Investigation to the Juárez cemetery, waited for exhumation of the executed men, and confirmed their identities. Despite a valid reason for optimism at diffusing some cause of the tension, Cobb's report of his actions to Secretary Lansing on January 24 concludes with a pessimistic view.

> *Confidentially:* The race feeling was apparent, and the feeling which we experienced was creepy.
>
> The conditions are becoming more difficult here. I am growing more afraid that things may break loose and get beyond control any time.
>
> As seen from here, the Carranza authorities have lost their opportunity to have established the trend toward improvement. The trend has set in against their success. As seen from here, I am reconciled to the expectation that conditions in the state of Chihuahua and along the border will grow worse.
>
> It is my judgment that our government must reconcile itself to the inability of success by the deserving elements in Mexico, and must reconcile itself to the necessity of directing a solution. I have delayed writing this, so as to endeavor not to be influenced by the recent abnormal conditions.[10] (Emphasis in original.)

Cobb thus saw the narrow window of opportunity for Carranza and Mexico close.

Cobb received a surprisingly quick response from Lansing in a highly personal letter of January 29, providing State's position and unsolicited praise.

In connection with your confidential opinion of the situation, I assure you that the situation is one of grave concern and that it will call for the exercise of all your tact and prudence.

The department is aware from the evidence furnished by your work and from statements of people who know you, that *you are an indefatigable* and conscientious worker, and I wish to thank you for the many proofs which the Department has had of your loyalty and zeal, and for the tireless manner in which you have labored to serve its best interests. I hope you will continue to be watchful and alert.

For some time your work has been in an *environment of criticism* and you will therefore appreciate that it is very necessary to be careful so that *no one can accuse you of being over zealous.*[11] (Emphasis added.)

Lansing's strengthening of ties with Cobb, so recently loosened, reflects more than sympathy with Cobb's expressed concern for the situation in El Paso and Mexico, which present but one side of a coin—with Germany on the other.

On January 21, a few days prior to his confidential observations to Lansing, Cobb advised Washington of an alleged meeting between Carranza and a German agent. At the meeting "arrangements were made for Germany to lend Carranza thirty-two officers and for Carranza to grant to Germany some certain peninsula south of Vera Cruz."[12] The information came from a local source, "C. P. Rodgers, a reputable lawyer of El Paso, [who] has been informed by an Englishman named Skates that one Angel Gutierrez" acted as interpreter.[13] While unable to confirm the meeting's agenda himself, Cobb knowingly noted who could: "Gutierrez, a man about twenty-six years old, can be found in San Antonio where he arrived from El Paso last night."[14] Although without the "stamp of reliability," State passed the message to Justice on January 24, "for such action as may be deemed appropriate," and, without Cobb's request, to the White House.[15] The president found the note interesting and asked, "Is the information it conveys not worth a very thorough investigation?"[16] Lansing eagerly, if inaccurately, responded on January 27.

> The matter has been referred to the Department of Justice for
> appropriate investigation by the Bureau of Investigation of the
> Department, and appropriate instructions to seek further infor-
> mation have been sent by the Department of State to the Collec-
> tor of Customs at El Paso.[17]

Cobb's reply from State, sent the next day, informed him of a Justice investigation and instructed him to "Informally and unoffi-
cially communicate to British consul, El Paso, and if possible secure
his cooperation in investigating report."[18] State did not pass on the
interest of the White House. Considering the timing of Lansing's
sympathetic and encouraging letter to Cobb and action of the German situation, Lansing may well have also had the German situation in mind as he responded to Cobb's Mexican concerns.

Detailed involvement with German activities would, for Cobb,
sit in limbo for some time, although he did rapidly respond, in a
message carelessly sent in plain text, to State's instructions reporting,
on February 6, local corroboration from the Bureau of Investigation
and the British consul.[19] Cobb acknowledged the reported meeting
as hearsay without the testimony of the still unlocated Gutiérrez.
State, admonishing Cobb to report in cipher, instructed him to
"Keep Department promptly informed of all developments."[20] No
new local development arose until April 20, when Cobb reported:

> I feel that Germany, either officially or as individuals, are mix-
> ing into our Mexican troubles, but without proof. Dare not take
> the responsibility of making the charge. I would like to under-
> take the duty of going to the bottom of these indications. Is
> there any way, without interference with other Departments,
> but in a way supplemental to their work, that the President
> might authorize me to secretly employ a few men, without
> knowledge of anyone else here, to work under me in the effort
> to get at this important truth.[21]

Such a request, if authorized, would take Cobb deeper into the
realm of intelligence as he would supervise a formal network of

paid agents to report specific information. He would then become
a professional intelligence officer.

State responded affirmatively four days later adding only a
caveat that such agents "not operate in United States territory."[22]
Despite such authorization and early awareness of the need not to
interfere with other competing agencies, nothing occurred on this
front until October.

Timing of concern with German intrigue and suggestions of
using secretly employed men to obtain information coincided with
similar action in the Department of State. Secretary Lansing had
long expressed concern with German activities in the United
States and Latin America, particularly in Mexico, and a need for
secret investigations to frustrate them. The growth and development of secret operations within the State Department during this
period has not received detailed investigation from historians.
Lansing's general account still provides the best summary and
insight into its development and function.

> The Secret Service of the Department of State was an orga-
> nization of slow growth during the period when this country
> was neutral. Prior to that time the Department had had no
> Secret Service. It was found necessary for the Department to
> conduct some investigations of a highly confidential character
> and for this purpose a few operatives of other departments were
> detailed to it. Agents were also employed in other countries,
> which necessitated an office in the Department to issue instruc-
> tions to them and to digest and analyze their reports without
> their going through the regular channels of departmental corre-
> spondence. In order to systematize this work at home and
> abroad Leland Harrison, one of the diplomatic secretaries, was
> in April, 1916, designated to take charge of the collection and
> examination of all information of a secret nature coming into
> the Department from various sources and also to direct the
> work of agents specially employed for that purpose.
>
> Under Mr. Harrison's efficient management and the gen-
> eral supervision of Mr. Polk, the Counselor for the Department,
> the Bureau of Secret Intelligence of the Department of State

grew to be a valuable adjunct to the government in the conduct of its international affairs. It was an independent bureau organized without sanction of law and had no legal standing, although it was nominally connected with the Division of Information, one of the regular divisions of the Department of State. As a result this extra-legal bureau was relatively small, and much of our information was obtained from other services and many of the investigations desired by the Department of State were made by operatives of such services. Our own agents in the capitals of the Allies were also aided materially by intelligence officers of the Allied Governments, who were only too willing to disclose their knowledge of German plots and intrigues, as for example in the case of the Zimmermann telegram.[23]

Without previous formal experience for guidance, Lansing hit on several key elements of intelligence in his statement. He established special communications channels for control and tasking and as a means for rudimentary analysis of incoming information. Noticeably lacking was a specific method of developing requirements to drive intelligence collection.

In the intervals between concerns over Germany, events in Mexico would proceed. On March 9, the incident Cobb had so long feared and generally prophesied arrived. Villa thundered across the border and raided the town of Columbus, New Mexico. Cobb's involvement with this episode falls into three broad categories, each of which deserves review. First came events prior to the raid, particularly information from Cobb regarding Villa's location and intentions; second, Cobb's reports, sources, and recommendations in the immediate aftermath of the raid; and finally, Cobb's support to the Pershing Expedition sent in pursuit of Villa.

In the months preceding the raid, Cobb had tracked the movements of Villa with interest and intensity. One aspect of Cobb's reporting deserves special attention; it approaches Villa's execution of and motivation for the raid, and United States reaction, from an informed contemporary viewpoint. Historians have put forth a number of reasons for the raid ranging from the more obvious revenge against the United States for recognizing Carranza and deserting Villa to German machinations distracting the United States from the war in Europe and simple revenge on Villa's part for the dishonesty of a local merchant.[24] Generally historians have dismissed or ignored reports of Villa fleeing to the United States as simply poor reporting or a distraction. Cobb's reporting of this possibility indicates a more elaborate situation.

On December 9, 1915, contradicting press reports and from an "authoritative source," Cobb placed Villa thirty miles west of Madera in western Chihuahua on the Mexico Northwestern Railroad.[25] Later that day Cobb, based on a "reliable source," more specifically placed Villa in Dolores on the eighth and due to reach Madera the tenth, "affording railroad connection either to Chihuahua or Juárez."[26] Despite this surprising level of refinement in locational data, Villa's troop strength and intentions at this point remained uncertain.[27] In mid-December attention shifted to the movement of Villa's family through El Paso en route to Havana, Cuba.[28] Reportedly a vehement anti-Villista, Cobb extended "every respect and legal courtesy of the port" to the family, including Hipólito Villa, but especially to Villa's wife. In the latter case, such consideration acknowledged her "greater influence over Villa than any other individual and it may be hoped that her presence and good treatment in this country may be a restraining influence upon him there."[29] Apparently from the family, Cobb learned that "Villa personally intended moving south" with the implication of continuing the fight.[30]

Until late December, Villa still controlled Juárez, although his rapidly disintegrating forces, after the Sonora campaign, rendered this a tenuous possession. As negotiations over Juárez continued, Cobb reported the Carranza consul's belief that "Villa's coming north with view to crossing to the United States and quitting rather than go south to fight."[31] Cobb reinforced this possibility several more times over the next few days and on December 20, reported:

There has been much talk of whether General Villa and his brother, Hipólito Villa, could enter the United States here without being arrested. Diverse parties have inquired of me to know especially as relates to criminal charges that might be filed for violation of customs laws. Feeling for the present that the broader advantage of eliminating them from Mexico is more important than the lesser advantage of prosecuting them I have referred all inquirers to General Pershing and Mr. Berkshire of Immigration Service, with bare statement that this office had no charges pending against them that would preclude their coming, thereby leaving open for future consideration by the Treasury Department question of whether they should be prosecuted for diamond smuggling.[32]

While Cobb artfully pushed responsibility off on others, he never objected to Villa's entry. The following day, again apparently based on information from the Villa family, Cobb reported:

General Villa supposed to be in mountains of Chihuahua but expected to follow family to Havana. Exact information as to whereabouts and intentions of General Villa unknown.[33]

Despite some cause for uncertainty, the collapsing Villa forces in addition to a pattern of flight among many Villa subordinates, loss of Juárez, departure of the Villa family, and the Villas as the apparent source of information must have all backed up the impression and probability of Villa leaving Mexico.

The next day, December 22, as negotiations between Villa and Carranza representatives over Juárez wound down, Cobb observed:

[Hipólito] Villa left El Paso last night by Southern Pacific for New Orleans to join party my [Cobb's telegram, see above] December 21, 12 noon. Attorney for H. Villa informs me H. Villa had information that General Villa is in mountains off from [sic] Chihuahua with no intention of coming out.[34]

This contradiction of previous indications must have caused confusion, if not concern. Fortunately, at the end of December, in a report unvouched for as of reliable origin, Cobb tentatively placed Villa "at Buenaventura; in the Galena district of Western Chihuahua, a Mexico North Western Railroad [*sic*] point, and coming north with forty men."[35] The direction of march and so few men would imply a peaceful border crossing.

Reports on Villa's movements from January through March 1916, up to the Columbus raid, witnessed equally erratic tracking from a wider variety of sources that slowly and inexorably gained in precision. Carranza authorities provided Cobb information in early January indicating Villa crossing "to U.S. somewhere in Columbus, New Mexico district."[36] For the remainder of January and February, reports of Villa crossing the border abated. As a result of the Santa Ysabel killings, Cobb wired Washington on January 13 a revised opinion of recent events.

> Belief is growing here, in which I am inclined to concur, that Villa who is responsible for outrages occurring in State of Chihuahua had his family go to Cuba so their presence in the United States or on border would not serve to restrain him from such outrages.[37]

In addition to portraying the heat of the moment, this comment demonstrates the kernel of Cobb's continual skepticism. Based on a "Reliable source," possibly the Mexico Northwestern Railroad agent in Madera, Cobb advised Washington of two boxcars of previously cached Villa ammunition supplies in Guerrero, south of Madera.[38] Corroboration of Villa's last reported location came from Deputy Collector of Customs Riggs in Columbus. Mexican farmers from El Valle, on the Santa Maria River, and south of Casas Grandes, Mexico, reported Villa "going to San Andres or somewhere around that vicinity" about January 10.[39] At the end of January, the "Best Information obtainable [placed] Villa in or about Santa Clara Valley northwest of Chihuahua and within striking distance of either Central or Northwestern Railroad."[40]

At about the same time, rumor, not fact, "from party whose information is usually correct," in a private telegram from Chihuahua, had Villa captured at Hacienda San Geronimo.[41] The

American Mining and Smelting Company located Villa's headquarters "at the Cañon de Santa Clara, not far from the railroad
some 100 miles north of Chihuahua."[42] An unidentified American
company placed Villa near Parral on February 4, 1916.[43] Returning to Carranza authorities in early February, Cobb, in a series of
messages, reported Villa robbing a train north of Chihuahua City,
killing an embarked former compatriot, proceeding to Ojinaga on
the border, and subsequently north of Gallego moving toward
Juárez.[44] The later report noted, in recognition of Villa's intelligence capabilities: "Telegraph wires not cut by Villa who is probably tapping them for information."[45]

In another view of this incident, Friedrich Katz, a historian of
the Mexican Revolution, relates "that Villa decided to attack Presidio, Texas [across from Ojinaga], but changed his mind after part
of his forces deserted."[46] Accepting this, and noting Cobb's assessment of Villa's use of the telegraph wires for intelligence, a tentative conclusion can be reached. Villa may have known from wiretaps of deserters revealing his plan as Carranza authorities knew
of his Ojinaga destination, although apparently not his possible
intention to cross the border on arrival. Such subtle intelligence
and communications efforts may explain how such disparate individuals acted in seeming harmony on this occasion. Returning to
the chase, on February 21 Cobb placed Villa near Cusihuiriachic, a
mining town west of Chihuahua City on the Northwestern
Railroad, with information from a "Reliable arrival from Chihuahua."[47]

Reports from December 1915 through the end of February
1916 had tracked Villa with a variety of sources. Villa's path seems
somewhat aimless. In early March, Villa's road to Columbus
became very clear in Cobb's reports. On March 3, from an
unknown source, Cobb returned to the theme of Villa peacefully
crossing the border to the United States and reported:

Villa left Pecheco Point, near Madera Wednesday [March 1] with
three hundred men headed toward Columbus, New Mexico. He
is reported west of Casagrades [*sic*] today. There is reason to

believe he intends to cross to United States and hopes to proceed
to Washington. Please consider this possibility and the necessity
of instructions to us on the border.[48]

State did not issue any instructions and Cobb did not appear to see
any incongruity between peaceful crossing and a force of more
than three hundred men. Three days later Cobb confirmed this
information and his link in Columbus.

My March 3, 2 p.m. [above] seems confirmed. Commanding
General [Gabriel] Gavira in Juárez announced this morning
that Villa was proceeding to border and that he asked American
military authorities to be on lookout for him. My tip is that he is
due tonight or tomorrow. I have instructed deputy at Columbus
[Riggs] to rush any information.[49]

Deputy Collector Riggs tested his telephone communications with
El Paso and Cobb the next day, reporting: "Villa with an estimated
four hundred men is on river south-east of Columbus, fifteen
miles west and fifty odd miles south."[50] In two messages on March
8, Cobb mused about the lack of Carrancista military action
against Villa, noting: "If Villa is permitted to remain in the open as
at present, without efficient action by Carranza forces, it will
encourage border opposition to Carranza and tend greatly to
undermine *de facto* Government."[51] State agreed with this general
assessment in a telegram to representatives near the Carranza government in Mexico calling this a "most serious situation."[52] Cobb
sent his final pre-raid communication on March 8, mailing an
unrelated letter to State which reflected some degree of unconcern
with Villa near the border.[53]

Beyond reinforcing the variety of Cobb's sources, his tracking
of Villa indicates both surprising consistency and inconsistency.
Cobb reported on Villa whenever information permitted. The
information more accurately reports Villa's movements than any
other source. Yet curiously, Cobb expressed no protectionist alarm
at Villa's presence along the border or objection to Villa's potential

entry into the United States. Perhaps, combined with his treatment of the Villa family, even if self-serving, Cobb's interest went beyond Villa himself and centered on the resolution of the situation, not any personal vendetta. Even after Santa Ysabel, Cobb did not express any vitriolic sentiment against Villa. Another perplexing reaction to Villa's presence on the border appears in Cobb's acceptance, on the one hand, of Villa crossing peacefully and, on the other, his faulting the Carranza authorities for not pursuing Villa. Additionally, Cobb's unexplained sources bear some examination. They seem to indicate, at times, a source close to Villa, exploitation of available technical communications in the form of telegraphy, or a combination of both. The former appears questionable in view of Cobb's supposed anti-Villista attitude and unlikely since Cobb failed continually to report any detail of Villa's internal decisions such as those reached at San Geronimo. For the latter, further speculation requires examination of additional reporting.

Cobb's reporting of the raid, because of its nature as a professional and first report to Washington, would earn him credit in today's intelligence system. Cobb's initial report, which he properly attributed to Deputy Collector Riggs's probable telephone call from Columbus and Department of Justice information, presents an accurate outline of the incident—time, location, friendly civilian and military casualties, destruction of property, hostile casualties and command structure, and friendly follow on action. In full, the report read:

> March 9, 9 a.m.
> Following from Deputy Collector, Columbus, New Mexico:
> Columbus attacked this morning, four thirty o'clock. Citizens murdered. Repulsed about six o'clock. Town partly burned. They have retreated to west. Unable to say how many were killed. Custom force and families O.K." [sic—no open quotes]
> Department of Justice informed that between four and five hundred Villa troops attacked Columbus, New Mexico, about four-thirty. Villa probably in charge. Three American soldiers

killed and several injured; also killed four civilians and wounded four. Several of attacking partly [*sic*] killed and wounded by our forces. Attacking party also burned depot and principal buildings in Columbus, United States soldiers now pursuing attacking parties across the line into Mexico. No prisoners reported taken alive. [Received in Washington at 1:35 p.m.][54]

Cobb, with direct access to Washington, reported promptly to State, who then obtained confirmation from Justice about thirty minutes later. Lansing then conferred with Secretary of War Newton D. Baker.[55] War apparently did not receive notice of the attack until later because of miscommunications between the telegrapher and the local commander in Columbus. Based on Cobb's report, State instructed U.S. Consul John R. Silliman, accompanying Carranza on a tour of Mexico's northern states, to urge the first chief to "do everything in his power to pursue, capture, and exterminate this lawless element which is now proceeding westward from Columbus."[56]

Over the next four days Cobb continued to provide additional information to Washington. An hour after first notifying Washington, he advised them of coordination between Deputy Collector Riggs and Associated Press correspondent George L. Seese in Columbus and the probable accuracy of the latter's reports.[57] This gave additional credence to press reports reaching Washington. Next, Cobb reported Villa's retention of extra mounts at his camp prior to the attack and, also, from Deputy Riggs:

> Villa was identified by a witness reporting to him as being in fighting at Columbus and that their rally cry was reported to him by those who claim to have heard it as being in Spanish: "Murder Americans viva Mexicans."[58]

Cobb, while previously seeing intervention in terms of the responsibility or irresponsibility of the Carranza government and not as a rabid interventionist, called for intervention as a military obligation and a matter of national honor.

It is the duty of our Government to now require respect for our people. National honor can make no stronger appeal than is now made that our people shall not be forsaken.

To get Villa we must send troops in after him. This will add to the tendency already created by his act this morning to make him a national hero. Therefore we may as well now meet the obligation, to which we must be reconciled, of taking positive hold of and solving the Mexican problem in its entirety. By an evasive course we would aggravate the problem. By meeting it, as is our duty, positively and with strength of action we will find that the Mexican people, in their own misery, would not seriously resist civilized intervention. Employing with wages paid in honest money would solve the biggest problem. The Mexican people would become reconciled to this being afforded by our Government as we must become reconciled to affording it.[59]

The record does not indicate Washington's reaction to such bold and unsolicited advice from a collector or an agent.

Returning to more practical matters, subsequent reports filled in details of the raid. Mrs. Riggs provided the names of the dead and wounded in addition to identifying the buildings destroyed, upon her arrival in El Paso.[60] Additional names of the dead and circumstances of their deaths followed in a final report of the day.[61] Other subordinates, their wives, and a captured Villa soldier provided information as to Villa's strength which ranged from three to four hundred in the attack and from two to three thousand in reserve. From the Carranza consul, Cobb reported Mexican troops moving against Villa and escorting the remaining Mormons out.[62] Additionally, Cobb reported another apparent violation of the border attributed to Villa, a raid near Mimbres, New Mexico, with two killed and horses stolen. Other reports included the cutting of telegraph wires near Corralitos, Carranza troops moving south from Chihuahua, not north (sourced from a "Mexican conductor"), and, from a captured diary at Columbus, Villa's route prior to the raid.[63]

Cobb's initial and subsequent detailed reports may have added weight to his more rational opinions and observations, which he also provided. On March 10, he recommended pursuing Villa from El Paso using the "North Western railroad [*sic*] for double purpose of protecting Mormon colonies, over four hundred men, women and children, against massacre and at same time to cut off Villa's retreat to mountains."[64] Later, three hours after advising of additional Mexican troop movements, Cobb further reported:

> Indications are that Carranza authorities will resent American troops entering Mexico. They are rushing troops to Juárez (my March 10 5P) I think as predicate to claim ours unnecessary. Ours are necessary.[65]

Recognizing the easing of the immediate crisis, Cobb volunteered to Washington a characterization of his efforts as "endeavoring to render every assistance possible to our military authorities especially transmitting all information worth while to General Pershing."[66]

Cobb's reporting during the crisis reflects the submission of timely and accurate information under the circumstances. His *ad hoc* system for providing timely information had worked well. Considering the activity Cobb's first message generated in Washington, his subsequent reports and opinions may have contributed to the decision-making process. Since the decision to intervene occurred on March 10, messages after that date had little impact. Cobb had reported and continued to reliably report Villa's movements and intentions. Meanwhile, the army maintained "he can strike at any point on the border comma [*sic*] we being unable to obtain advance information as to his whereabouts."[67] Vitriolic statements chastising Villa, speculation regarding the raid's motivation, and Villa's failure to cross the border peacefully are surprisingly absent from Cobb's reports. With the infusion of U.S. Army forces to the border and an influx of other federal agents, his role increasingly became that of one among many more. Despite the competition, he continued to provide information to Washington even if such service lacked the tensions of a Huerta arrest, local embargo, or cross-border raid.

Cobb presented no direct comment regarding Villa's motivation for the raid. An element of motivation surfaces, however, in Cobb's reporting which others have ignored. Friedrich Katz saw the primary reason as "Villa's firm belief that Woodrow Wilson had concluded an agreement with Carranza that would virtually convert Mexico into a U.S. protectorate."[68] Katz also believed that, after the failed attempt to raid Ojinaga/Presidio, "Villa became extremely reserved about the name of the town he planned to attack. It was only when they arrived near Columbus, New Mexico, that his men found out where they were going."[69] But this ignores the paucity of targets on the Chihuahua–United States border and Cobb's reporting of the destination as early as March 3, well prior to Villa's arrival on the border. Additionally, lingering near the border and the isolated town of Columbus for several days violates any precepts of security. Villa's rumored peaceful crossing could represent a well organized deception; however, while capable of a tactical ruse, a deception of this depth appears beyond Villa's organization at the time.

The persistence of the rumor and its various sources makes surface dismissal simplistic. Cobb's suspicious nature and at least a lack of support for Villa render him a poor candidate to easily accept a fallacious rumor. Also, Cobb had previously predicted a probable cross-border action, indicating he at least recognized the possibility. Based on Cobb's reporting and subsequent events, Villa could have approached the border with two options: hostile or peaceful crossing. Or perhaps, as some element of motivation, Villa needed to crush rumors of departure—to close the door to the United States in more than one way—to survive as a guerrilla in Mexico. Since the question of Villa's very presence at Columbus still engenders speculation from historians and Villa never directly confirmed or denied his role, his options and motivations prior to the raid, based on contemporary reporting, bear consideration.

Early reports from Cobb probably provided the army a valuable additional source of information regarding Villa and events in Mexico. Initially, reports tentatively placed Villa near Corralitos based on severed telegraph lines in the area. Cobb, however, expressed more concern with alternative telegraphic communications routes to the area. With the restoration of the lines two days later, on March 14, the day prior to Pershing's entry into Mexico at Columbus, Cobb reported Villa's strength at about three hundred and location as "south of Corralitos and north of Casas Grandes last night."[70] This came from a Villa deserter in Casas Grandes. The report continued with the supposition, based on "later information" contained in the same telegram and possibly from a second source, that Villa "broke camp and started south at five o'clock this morning along foothills about five miles northeast of Casasgrandes [sic] . . . [and] is headed toward Colonia Juárez."[71] Two days later Cobb reported, without noting his source, details of Villa's actions around Corralitos, movement toward Galeana, the size of his supply train, and written communications to Carranza authorities in Casas Grandes.[72] Pershing may have based his force's initial objective of Casas Grandes in part on this information.

At the end of March, Cobb's continued reporting earned him an additional responsibility from Washington. State instructed the U.S. consul in Chihuahua, Marion Letcher, to report any Villa movements to Cobb for further transmission to the army.[73] This simple administrative solution provided rapid support to the army. Unfortunately, another more technical communications problem existed. Cobb could report to Washington Villa's location at Mal Pass, "a station on Northwestern Railroad lying between La Junta and San Antonio [Mexico] and northwest Cusi," and could pass the information to local authorities for General Funston in San Antonio, Texas.[74] He could not wire the information directly to Funston "unless you [State] furnish him State Department code or he can furnish me army code."[75] Cobb's local solution came the next day: "Am providing office on my floor in Federal Building for use military commanders here. This will enable prompt relay messages to General Funston."[76] In modern terms, between this communication and coordination arrangement, information from Chihuahua, and his own sources, Cobb had established a rudimentary joint

*Looking north on Oregon Street in the 1910s with the trees of
San Jacinto Plaza in the background and the tower of the Federal Building
right center. Texas Street enters from the right.
Cobb undoubtedly used the Western Union outlet located
on the ground floor of the building on the left
to send and receive his telegrams.
(Courtesy of the University of Texas at El Paso
Library, Special Collections.)*

intelligence center. Unfortunately, messages passed between Cobb and the army via this system have not, as yet, been located.

Pershing, in the mountains of Mexico, came much closer to Villa than Cobb in an office in El Paso. Nonetheless, highlights of Cobb's service to Pershing provide some items of interest. Cobb's minor obsession, particularly during April 1916, seemed to center on Villa's wound initially reported by army officers in Mexico on March 25.[77] Nine days later, from a Mexican traveler whose information seemed "usually reliable but cannot be checked or guaranteed," Cobb reported Villa heading toward Parral via Satevo but the "Informant also states Villa has not been wounded."[78] This contradicted an earlier message relayed from the U.S. consul in Chihuahua confirming Villa's wound.[79] Three hours later "telegraphic information just received from reliable source" confirmed Villa's route but reported Villa wounded in the knee.[80] On April 11, in a private letter from Chihuahua dated April 4, came information of a more romantic cause for the wound.[81] Not until July 5 would Cobb return to the subject, reporting confirmation of Villa's location at Rosario below Parral and

> that Villa's wounds were caused by bullet that passed through the back muscles of both thighs without striking a bone and that Villa has sufficiently recovered to walk with a limp and to ride with greater ease.[82]

Reflecting more than simple confusion, these messages illustrate the difficulty in obtaining valid information from Mexico and the skepticism with which Cobb approached information and sources. In a final illustration of Cobb's skepticism, when rumors surfaced in mid-April of Villa's death due to his wounds, Cobb consulted with local doctors to determine if the wound could have caused death in the manner rumored. He also obtained from a local dentist, P. G. Sayer, a technical description of Villa's bridgework to positively identify the body.[83]

Although Pershing would remain in Chihuahua until February 5, 1917, and incidents at Parral and Carrizal would bring the two nations to the brink of war, Cobb played a relatively small role in the pursuit of Villa or collateral diplomacy. As an example, despite State sponsorship, Cobb made no comment on the talks between Generals Scott, Funston, and Obregón in El Paso after the April 12 incident at Parral.[84] Once the expedition entered Mexico, and despite his communications arrangements, Cobb concentrated more on related border events. This may reflect instructions Cobb received while visiting Washington in May 1916; however, no record or mention of the details of the trip survive.[85] Or the paucity of significant support to military operations may reflect Cobb's realization of the political nature of the expedition after Carrizal. During the expedition, Cobb sent Washington more than 450 messages and letters. The majority of these cover political and financial affairs in Mexico with an additional thread of interest in German involvement there.

As a politician, Cobb well recognized the political aspects of the incursion into Mexico. He provided his opinion in a single long sentence to Washington on March 22, after Pershing crossed the border.

> I respectfully report the conviction that our Government, in recognition of the fact that Mexico is dominated by conditions and not by the inadequate Carranza Government, must be reconciled to the duty, not alone to American rights, but as well to the rights of the Mexican people themselves, of solving the Mexican problem in its entirety: by policing with our military so far as necessary in order to give nature a chance to work its cure that employment, real money and confidence may combat the ignorance, official corruption, typhus and growing famine now oppressing their people and destroying their country.[86]

Cobb envisioned more than Pershing or Washington ever expected to deliver. Cobb believed the Carranza authorities incapable of fulfilling the basic obligations of government. In early June, he would report:

> Situation in Chihuahua desperate, due to extreme economic conditions and Government effort to divert attention by agitation

against Americans. . . . It is more probable that *de facto* Government in Chihuahua will collapse and that we will be confronted with a new organization in control but nominally with the same impossible conditions in control actually.[87] (Emphasis in original.)

In late 1916, nepotism, graft, and corruption characterized state and local government in Chihuahua. Dominating the scene were two competing families: the Treviños, prevailing in Chihuahua, and the Herreras, controlling Parral and Juárez. Each appeared more interested in profiting at the expense of local merchants and absentee American mine owners than in pursuing Villa.[88] According to Cobb, "graft so thoroughly dominates the state of Chihuahua, and jealousy among the grafters is so great that disintegration is indicated. Their official [*sic*] are grafters without shame."[89]

Of equal importance in Cobb's reporting, information on financial and commercial affairs in Mexico surfaces. Characteristic of his interest, on March 25 Cobb provided State with a summary of the Banco Nacional, Villista, and Carrancista currencies from 1913 to date.[90] In the following months, Cobb's reporting on exportation of gold for personal profit, exploitation of merchants, destruction of trade, and devaluation of paper currency outlined a collapsing economy. "The use of paper money," he would relate in October 1916, "is being gradually abandoned, and its value is already nearly gone."[91] In January 1917, Mexican soldiers received their pay in U.S. currency.[92] Simultaneously, gold, silver, and other valuables funneled from the country.[93] Merchants in Mexico received so much blame for rising prices that they closed their doors in protest of both their innocence and government regulation.[94]

In all this upheaval, Cobb sympathized with the suffering and plight of the Mexican people.

Mexican peon arrivals from interior bring distressing evidence of suffering, in the hunger and sickness that appears to prevail from Chihuahua as far south as San Luis Potosi, Aguas Calientes [*sic*] and Zacatecas, particularly in camps and smaller towns.[95]

Cobb failed to see in the details and human suffering the necessary revolutionary destruction of the old order and the birth of a new society as seen by historians. One leading historian of the Mexican Revolution, Alan Knight, observed:

> The inflation thus contributed significantly to the social change set in motion by the Revolution, whose effects were generally redistributive and leveling; certainly it helped further erode the positions of the old propertied, Porfirian elite, already buffeted by five years of civil war. Inflation, and the opportunities which went with it, also stimulated the entrepreneurialism and economic innovation of those years.[96]

Despite the volume and breadth of his reporting, Cobb still received occasional requests for information from State. Evaluation of food production and possible famine in Mexico came to State's attention in September 1916.[97] In response to their request for information on conditions in northern Mexico, Cobb provided, in five days, a detailed six-page, crop-by-crop report.[98] State may have used this in part as a potential "lever to control the Carranza regime."[99] Conflicting and exaggerated reports of events in Chihuahua frequently surfaced in press stories from El Paso. State received a request to clarify the situation from the Joint Mexican-American Commission, meeting in New London, Connecticut, to discuss Pershing's withdrawal after the incident at Carrizal. Accordingly, State instructed Cobb and its two official representatives on the border, Carothers and Thomas Edwards, the consul in Juárez, to report on the situation and explain "if possible why such stories are being disseminated, and with whom they originate."[100] Edwards reported "a concerted action by the press and public to baffle the Joint Commission," and to provide income to Mexicans and Americans by maintaining the army along the border and in Mexico.[101] Carothers responded, assigning responsibility for the stories to refugees and describing events in Chihuahua.[102] Cobb, in a detailed and comprehensive report, described the anti-Carranza sentiment in Chihuahua and Villa's continuing popularity, attributing the stories to Villistas and Americans eager to share in renewed loot.[103] The three responses may not have clarified the situation for State or the Joint Commission, but Cobb's stood as the most coherent and responsive.

Intervention did not increase or dramatically change the nature of Cobb's reporting. Columbus, and to a lesser extent the Pershing Expedition, would represent Cobb's last nationally significant crisis along the border. Occasionally, State would request specific information from him but, in general, it seemed satisfied with the level and diversity of his reports. His varied subjects reflected the wide assortment of his sources. One side of his net reported from public sources—newspapers and associated reporters, his own customs records and employees, Mexican officials, and banking reports. Another side seems to reflect an openness and affability in dealing with people across the economic, political, social, and cultural spectrum. Travelers, managers of companies with interests in Mexico, railway workers, personal contacts with Mexican government employees, and casual acquaintances all contributed to a directory from which Cobb extracted as needed. Cobb rarely attached names to his sources and normally requested that their identities receive protection even when provided. As an example of Cobb's ability and attitude toward people and information, he reported this background to State:

> On Sunday, February 20th, I was talking to an El Paso merchant, with whom I had frequently talked for the purpose of getting whatever information could be obtained from him upon Mexican matters. He has been an El Paso confidant of Manuel Calero, and in the past I have obtained considerable information from him originating with that particular group of Mexicans.[104]

On occasion, the mystery of sources and the speed with which accurate and timely information materialized indicate the use of Mexican telegraphers or at least some aspect of the system at Cobb's disposal. No evidence at this point indicates that Cobb had routine access to such sources. He used American companies and their often coded reports, travelers' comments, and direct reports, along with donated letters and telegrams, perhaps sometimes surreptitiously obtained, as primary sources.

Cobb's impact as an agent of influence on policy and diplomacy shrank with the raid on Columbus, while his role as a provider of information increased and showed indications of professionalization. Although Cobb could still influence public opinion and expectations along the border, as in the Akers murder crisis, the incident at Columbus presented far too large a crisis for one man to address. The raid brought increased levels of attention and activity to the border and degraded even further the ability of a single individual to influence events. Attention and crisis also resulted in the increasing importance of information. With authorization to employ agents across the border, Cobb stood on the verge of professional responsibilities. While the scope of information never narrowed, with agents and associated guidance from Washington, the focus on the German activities nonetheless increased. With American entry into the war in Europe, different opportunities and requirements would demand different methods.

CHAPTER FOUR

German Operations and Professionalism

CONCERN FOR BORDER SECURITY still existed in 1917 as Villa continued to roam Chihuahua at will and Carranza's government battled against relentless banditry. Fortunately, no significant crisis agitated fears of war between Mexico and the United States. Carranza concentrated on the struggle to ensure his survival and the success of the February 5, 1917, constitution as the basis for Mexico's future. With Pershing's withdrawal on February 5, and U.S. entry into the war in Europe in April, Wilson's policy pursued a modicum of respect for Mexican sovereignty. In an environment without a distracting crisis, but with additional requirements and challenges, Cobb honed his skill as an intelligence agent. Four issues agitated Mexican-U.S. relations. Historian Edward P. Haley has noted three: "Mexican oil, Mexican neutrality and the new Mexican constitution with its provisions that threatened foreign interests." But he omitted a fourth, German activities in Mexico.[1] Mexican oil, centered in Tampico and the Mexican states of Tamaulipas and Veracruz, fell beyond

Cobb's reach to routinely provide information. Neutrality and property rights, for Cobb, found expression in terms of German business and political intrigue in Chihuahua and in general reporting on Mexico's financial and economic health. Within these unspectacular confines, Cobb operated in closer coordination with other intelligence agencies along the border. To augment his more incidental sources, he developed a network of subordinate agents routinely supplying information on selected targets. Continuing whispers and indications of German involvement in Mexican affairs peppered his reports and sustained Washington's concern with border events.

Cobb's sources in late 1916 and early 1917 bear continuing comment. In general, Americans fled Mexico in the wake of the Columbus raid, the clash at Parral in April 1916, and growing anti-U.S. sentiment with the lingering presence of Pershing in Mexico. In addition to his usual sources, reporters, travelers, friends, and casual acquaintances, Cobb increasingly relied upon foreigners, particularly British subjects, and especially British consuls.[2] By November 1916, his contacts and communications system within Chihuahua led the Department of State to request Cobb to relay a message to the British consul at Chihuahua for the British embassy in Washington.[3]

Despite authorization to employ agents against the Germans in Mexico, little real evidence of their use emerges in Cobb's earlier reports. In late 1916, Cobb surprisingly allowed an insight into this more professional operation which had grown with the passage of time. Prior to his trip to Washington in November 1916, he provided the status of his expenditures to date, $1,914.40, for his agents.[4] His primary agent, H. J. Baron "of the Mexican Chemical Company at Chihuahua" received $75.00 for general services, $4.00 for couriering the message to the British consul in Chihuahua, and $3.00 for providing copies of the Mexican paper *El Democratas*.[5] Cobb paid A. H. Davidson $75.00 for his services in investigating ammunition smuggling, and H. N. Gray, the "local chief of Carranza secret services," $25.00.[6] Billy Smith received $10.00 for unspecified duties, and Mexican laborers earned $2.40

for searching suspicious coal cars for ammunition. Cobb would employ several more agents in Mexico, but this provides the single most insightful look into his network.

As the year progressed, a certain amount of cynicism entered into Cobb's evaluation of potential sources, agents, and allies. He regarded Andrés García, the Mexican director of consulates, as particularly untrustworthy and dishonest, although such a man could prove useful. Cobb advised Washington of his attitude.

> I wish the Department to understand that García is thoroughly corrupt, as has been set forth in various reports, and that any action he takes against German interests and favorably to American interests will be for some ulterior purpose, perhaps to cover up his former rascality and endeavor to gain favor with a view to future schemes. However, if he is working against the Germans, and to that extent in favor of Americans, we may as well use him.[7]

Cobb demonstrated a measure of pragmatism which can also mark a professional case officer.

Another measure of his professionalism comes in the use that the State Department made of selected reports from El Paso. Increasing numbers of items were forwarded to the U.S. embassy in Mexico for information or comment. Cobb received full credit as the source. No specific theme or significant event emerges from the coordinated reports, which advised of German activity along the border, German-Mexican relations in Chihuahua, proposed changes of Carranza personnel along the border, shipment of propaganda material from Mexico to the United States, and possible German exclusion from the border area within Mexico.[8] In this manner, Cobb had a small role in the developing coordinated international intelligence system in the State Department.

His concerns with Germany had lain dormant since August 1916.[9] Suddenly, in late December, commensurate with his emerging network, the German investigation had risen again and required State action to ensure its success. Cobb advised Washington of an army intelligence investigation under Brigadier General George Bell, the local commander at Fort Bliss, "jeopardizing investigation for you [State]. Can you not please have War Department direct him to abstain while covering subject for you?"[10] The subject of the investigation stood as the recent expansion in Mexico of the German mining firm, Frankfurter Metallgesellschaft.[11] State's interest caused a request to the Department of War to suspend temporarily its efforts and instructions to Cobb to rush his report.[12] Cobb dutifully responded on January 11, indicating a complex situation requiring caution "to keep from exciting mining men too much" and suggesting "additional information might be gotten at Los Angeles, San Antonio, Laredo, Eagle Pass and Mexico itself."[13] Washington recognized this as indicative of a long and extensive investigation. In two messages the following day, State rescinded its request to the Department of War and directed Cobb to coordinate with the army and the Bureau of Investigation to ensure "such perfect understanding and co-operation between you three as will prevent any unnecessary duplication of work in connection with this and other similar investigations."[14]

Some historians have unjustly characterized Cobb's initial message regarding army interference as a constant complaint on his part and an indicator of continual conflict among U.S. intelligence agencies along the border.[15] A single message hardly constitutes a perpetual lament and, viewed in context, the State Department quickly corrected any opportunity for uncoordinated action. In general, Cobb's previous actions and procedures consistently provided for close coordination with other agencies. Nonetheless, Cobb then redoubled his efforts at coordination and cooperation.[16] In this particular case he protested his possible elimination from the investigation and advised Washington of his dependence for information "upon confidence of friends the most important of whom said he refused General's Bells [sic] request for such information upon express instructions of his company."[17] Additionally, this exception may have found motivation in Cobb's distress over Mexican perceptions of General Bell's possible exercise of diplomatic authority with regard to deporting selected aliens.[18] In the absence of instructions to the contrary and in light of Cobb's specific efforts at coordination, he continued to investigate German activities in Mexico, with unexpected dividends.

German intrigue in Mexico reached its public height with publication, in the New York morning papers, of the Zimmermann telegram on March 1, 1917.[19] The intercepted missive offered Mexico "the lost territory in Texas, New Mexico, and Arizona" in exchange for a wartime alliance against the United States.[20] On the afternoon of March 1, Cobb provided an unexpected confirmation and possible expansion of the offer.

> British friend from Parral apparently without any motive informs me confidentially [of] report from Mexican agent there that Villa left Parral February nineteenth with one thousand equipped and two thousand partially equipped men going west possibly intending to turn north, that in speeches by Villa at Parral and Santa Barbara, he stated he was "going to help Germans whip [the] United States and *obtain Texas, Arizona, and California back for Mexico* and those not contributing financially would have to serve as soldiers against Americans." As formerly reported, my belief Germans playing both Carranza and Villa against Americans with only occasional slips. British friend state [Carranza's military commander in Chihuahua, General Francisco] Murguía recently temporarily arrested German Consul and German merchant at Parral for having helped Villa.[21] (Emphasis added.)

Similarity of objectives and involvement of the Germans with a second Mexican faction creates obvious conclusions. At least one historian noted the impact of Cobb's report on official Washington.

> The coincidence of the wording with that of the Zimmermann telegram was too striking to be missed and indicated that the Germans must have made a similar proposition to Villa or that he had learned of it somehow.[22]

It may be speculated that the similarity may have had a greater relationship with individual survival and careful analysis of the needs of Mexican factions rather than with international intrigue and the crisis of the moment.

Since at least the summer of 1916, Cobb had given the Parral area and southwestern Chihuahua special attention. Three important elements met in the region: mining, Villa, and German interests. Ever open to opportunities to acquire valid information of interest to him, Cobb took an unusual approach in January 1917. He contacted the German vice consul from Parral.

> There has been so much suggestion of German influence behind Villa that I have watched for every opportunity to seek information upon the subject. As there was talk of the character that came from Parral, I watched particularly for a chance to talk with the German Vice Consul at Parral, Mr Edward Kock, upon one of his recent trips to El Paso, seeking an opportunity to draw him out, without any suspicion on his part. . . . He has been to the office three times to call, and on the last call we had a long talk, in which he did most of the talking, describing his experience as a prisoner of Villa, in detail, and with apparent truthfulness.[23]

After presenting Kock's view of Villa and his impressions of the situation in Mexico, Cobb's report closed with an informative anecdote.

> Finally, Mr. Kock made the very interesting statement that the local Carranza authorities at Parral, away back at the time of the Pershing troops were in that vicinity [April 1916], approached him as the German representative and sought that he apply to Germany for assistance to help them drive the Gringos from Mexican soil. He was amused at their ignorance in the matter, but frankly stated that he told them that he would seek such assistance for them.[24]

While no evidence exists that Kock subsequently provided similar assurances to Villa, Murguía did detain the vice consul at Parral for helping Villa. Neither Cobb nor State connected Villa's statement of February 19 and Kock's statements of early January. In a similar vein, Cobb expressed no surprise at Villa's presence in Parral on that date and his own inability to locate Villa at that time.[25] It would appear that agent, agency, and historians have accepted the report of the "British friend at Parral" at face value in light of the Zimmermann crisis rather than in the context of events on the border.

Among the previously noted network of agents and contacts in Mexico, Cobb's British friend would appear not as a casual acquaintance but rather a source he had carefully developed. Some seven months later, in September 1917, Cobb may have inadvertently identified him.

> My friend, Mr Harrison *(whose name must be protected)*, a British subject, and manager of the British company owning the San Francisco mines at Santa Barbara, near Parral, Chihuahua, Mexico. . . .[26] (Emphasis in original.)

Friendship, citizenship, and location all indicate that Harrison may have acted as Cobb's March 1 source in Parral.

As previously noted, Cobb's reports and presentation of the Germans in Mexico fueled concern, if not alarm, in Washington. His view of German activities, however, went beyond a simple alarmist mentality. Despite growing concern in the nation over Germany's conduct in Europe and its actions in Mexico, and despite his own suspicions, he continued to communicate openly with Germans on both sides of the border. Well prior to Wilson's signing the declaration of war against Germany on April 6, 1917, Cobb identified German economic involvement in Mexico as an area of primary concern.

> There is one phase of Mexican developments which, from the view-point of looking into the future, seems to me to be significant.
>   The Germans appear to be taking advantage of conditions in Mexico, and of our suspended American enterprise, to acquire property and to get into fields which it would be more to our interest to have developed by American capital.[27]

As his exposure to such activities in Mexico continued, Cobb developed an appreciation for German methods and objectives. In addition to acquiring property, they played both factions, Carrancista and Villista, against each other to sustain turmoil on the border. Cobb's most insightful commentary accompanied his report on German Vice Consul Kock.

> This incident [promising German aid], I think, goes to explain the German relation to the Mexicans: First, that it is more a case of Mexican ignorance in expecting assistance than of German intention of giving same; second, that the Germans taffy the Mexican authorities, whether Carrancista, Villista or otherwise, who happen to be in the locality at the time, in the course of playing all ends against the middle, for whatever may be to their commercial advantage; and, third, and finally, that the Germans are more interested in seeking their industrial and commercial advantage in Mexico than they are in helping the political fortune of any of the Mexicans.[28]

Insight provided little assistance in devising a solution to German economic penetration; Cobb merely reported acquisitions and industrial operations as they occurred.

In early 1917, German activities still held a secondary position to Cobb's primary interest—the situation in Mexico. As the fight against Villa continued in Chihuahua, both sides relied on the United States for ammunition. In October 1916, Cobb received permission from Washington to "use a secret man at State Department expense" to prevent ammunition smuggling.[29] As the year closed, reports indicated Villa's dwindling supply of ammunition.

> My friend Doctor Sigmund Haffner, whose name please protect, German citizen formerly of Chihuahua now of El Paso absolutely reliable, on train at Laguna October thirtieth, states to me in effect train stopped and assaulted by about two hundred Villistas. . . . Bandits equipped with guns and some ammunition but noticeably avoiding wasting ammunition. Haffner was saved by being recognized rather than being exempted as German.[30]

Shortage of ammunition drove demand, and as demand grew so did opportunity for profits. In January 1917 the border seemed to leak like a sieve and the Mexican authorities complained of a poorly enforced embargo.[31] While the various enforcement agencies provided mutual defense, Cobb devised an innovative solution.

> Recommend that all border railroads, so as to avoid refusals because of competition be requested from Washington to furnish government agents memoranda of ammunition shipments to border points, and as soon as consistent that either military or customs be authorized to seize ammunition intended for Mexico and already accumulated on border.[32]

Cobb reiterated and provided background to his proposal a few days later but, before its arrival, State, in coordination with War, indicated approval of his preliminary suggestion and requested specific suggestions for implementation.[33] Cobb responded on February 17 with the names of specific railroads to contact; State requested railroad cooperation on March 12.[34] As State obtained the concurrence of appropriate railroad presidents, a system of notification of ammunition shipments to the El Paso border area soon became a reality.[35]

Implementation of this program required further coordination and cooperation and, with some stubborn suppliers, an element of "bluff."[36] On March 15 Cobb reported, despite one or two holdouts among the local merchants, "Ammunition situation in better control than ever before."[37] Considering the timing of local actions and State's request for cooperation to the railroads, Cobb undoubtedly bluffed more than one local merchant and shipper. Success bred support from other agencies and recommendations for greater action.

> We, representing the three Departments [Justice, War, and Treasury], are working together in the matter, and are gratified in feeling that we have the ammunition situation at El Paso under better control now than ever before, although it could

> well be improved if the Departments at Washington could
> authorize us, or any of us, to prevent the distribution of ammu-
> nition held in the warehouse by large dealers here.[38]

State did not respond and Treasury referred action to local authorities as well as the departments of State, War, and Justice but let
stand arrangements with the railroad.[39] Cobb nonetheless
expected continuing success.

> I expect to be able to improve our control over the ammunition
> situation here. I think that I have the ammunition shippers
> bluffed off of the boards, and intend to so handle the matter as
> to give them no opportunity to call the bluff.[40]

Cobb certainly had applied lessons learned during the coal
embargo of 1915.

Success again bred support, this time in the form of imitation
and a recommendation for additional action. Pershing, transferred
to Fort Sam Houston as the Southern Department commander,
urged the War Department in early April to "refuse shipments [of]
arms and ammunition of any description to border points unless
shipments have approval of military authorities."[41] The Special
Committee on National Defense approved the recommendation
and Pershing issued implementing instructions on April 18.[42]
When notified, Cobb wrote to General Bell at Fort Bliss and
informed him of his own system, commended expansion and, in
an unusual diatribe, pointed out another element of the problem
beyond ammunition control.

> In the city of El Paso, we do not know how many former Villa
> bandit soldiers, former Orosco [sic] bandit soldiers, and perhaps,
> former Carranza bandit soldiers, walk our streets, apparently inno-
> cent and harmless peons, but actually a dangerous element,
> through the possession, in their homes, situated on American soil,
> of such guns, rifles, etc. We can never rest easy until the border is
> freed from this menace by a systematic disarming of such people.[43]

Cobb made similar appeals to Treasury and State in cover letters attached to his correspondence with General Bell. Fortunately, no one responded.

Having established an effective and even copied system, Cobb faced additional challenges to its success and utility. Based on confidential information from a local broker and a letter to the broker from a former chemist at the Mexican National Powder Works at Santa Fe, near Mexico City, Cobb reported in January 1917 on the operation and production of the plant.[44] In a follow-up report from the same sources, he quoted the chemist's reference to " 'secret chemicals' used in small amounts that I [the chemist] am under engagement not to reveal" and requested guidance from State pursuant to follow-up efforts in the matter.[45] In the absence of apparent instructions, Cobb nevertheless remained alert and, the following month, from a new source, reported a development at once alarming and encouraging. Based on the visit to Cobb's office of J. L. Gutiérrez, superintendent of the railroad from Ciudad Juárez to Torreón, Cobb learned:

> he was at Manzanillo about February 6th, by direction of General Obregón, to unload and forward by railroad, machinery received at that port from Japan; stating that there was machinery for the manufacture of ammunition [and uniforms]. He also added that eighty or ninety Japanese accompanied the machinery for the purpose of installing it at Mexico City.[46]

Acknowledging the man's naiveté and honesty rather than a second source as confirmation, Cobb quickly silenced any alarms over the revelation.

> The above information followed a statement by Sr. Gutiérrez of their great need for ammunition. I asked him how they could need ammunition so badly after having received machinery from Japan with which to manufacture same. He then disclosed the foregoing information, and also said that the machinery could not be installed within six months; that even then,

they would lack the raw materials from which to manufacture
munitions. And, further, that they were dependent for ammunition upon American sources of supply.[47]

This incident indicates the apparent paucity of guidance from
Washington, Cobb's recognition of valuable information, and the
affable nature needed to extract it from an opportune source without raising alarm. Indigenous manufacture of ammunition in
Mexico would have obviated an embargo and detracted from
efforts to influence events.

Prewar concerns with German activity in Mexico soon centered on one man—Francisco or Franz Gottwald. He surfaced initially in several ammunition smuggling operations pursuant to his
assignment as the chief commissary officer and paymaster for
General Murguía.[48] Originally reported as the manager of the
Toluca Brewery near Mexico City, he later was said to have been
"first employed in Chihuahua as a sort of instructor . . . in artillery
[and] has every appearance in personal bearing and manner of a
trained military officer."[49] Cooperation with local Justice agents
indicated a possible new means of tracking his operations.

> [Gottwald] ordering private telephone installed here [El Paso].
> Connecting phone might disclose German-Carranza local con-
> nections. Washington would have to arrange with New York
> Office Bell Telephone company for this privilege.[50]

State did not respond but Justice arrested Gottwald on April 5,
making State's response irrelevant.[51] Cobb assisted in Gottwald's
interrogation and confirmed association with the Carranza government but could only link the suspect circumstantially to German intrigue. Gottwald's dual German-Mexican citizenship
seemed to negate that avenue of attack.[52] Because Justice acted as
the government's primary agency in Gottwald's prosecution,
Cobb's role quickly marginalized. This did not prevent his raising
concerns and recommending courses of action to State. But with
Gottwald, in essence, neutralized, and the nation a wartime

combatant, other Germans attracted attention. Of course, Mexico also remained a point of attention.[53]

In the past, a variety of diverse subjects of possible interest to Washington, both critical and mundane, had surfaced in Cobb's reporting. Surprisingly, reports for the second half of 1917 and early 1918 found Mexico only as a critical backdrop. Villa's status, predictions of Carranza's downfall, and laments regarding the future of the nation subsided significantly, although Mexican government finances did remain a topic of interest, particularly the transfer of gold across the border. With great frequency Mexico imported and exported large sums of gold bullion and coins. Normally Cobb reported the arrival or departure, amount, probable purpose, and controlling authority of these shipments. Sometimes he expressed concern with regard to the graft Mexican officials made as a result of the transfers.[54] The secretary of the treasury noted a more ominous purpose, while seeking a diplomatic solution, in Cobb's innocuous reports.

> A. Iselin and Company have apparently been dealing in Mexican exchange, obtaining Mexican pesos along the Mexican border and selling them in Mexico. This source of supply was, of course, rather limited and A. Iselin and company, or some of their associates, conceived the idea of interesting the Mexican Government in the situation with a view to having the United States Government coin American gold into Mexican pesos, not for the Mexican Treasury Department, but for the purpose of profit to the bankers and the Mexican government by selling such gold at a premium in Mexico. Mr. Iselin told this Department that the proposition was initiated by his firm. . . . This contract was in the nature of a purely business transaction and the one indispensable agency to carry it into effect was the United States Mint. Its purpose was the large profits involved, which were made possible, first, by reason of the Mexican order regulating exchange, and, secondly, by reason of the fact that the coinage would have been executed at the United States Mint at cost.[55]

Cobb apparently received no notice of Treasury's action.[56]

In the political realm, Cobb made some minor reports on the Carranza-Obregón split but concentrated on the activities of Murguía. Cobb found him "a brute of the Villa type, in one particular case worse than Villa himself, in that Murguía is addicted to drunkenness."[57] This opinion seemed confirmed with reports of Murguía's brutality to his own subordinates and others.[58] While graft also may have influenced Cobb's opinion, Murguía's connection with Germans in Chihuahua undoubtedly played a larger role.

Previously, incidental German involvement in commercial, financial, and economic activities, even with regard to ammunition sales and smuggling, remained in the context of the overall Mexican problem. After entry into the war, Cobb understandably increased his reports on German activities but failed to speculate on their motivation. His country's hostility to that nation provided sufficient justification to suspect and report any actions. Little hint of racism or xenophobia surfaces in his German reports. They concentrated on valid activities of German citizens which, while not rampant, did see organization and planning in individual actions. German association with Mexican officials and propaganda within Mexico drew concern and attempts at solutions.

War created changes in the evaluation and treatment of the possible German threat. Initial actions against German border operations in Mexico appear disjointed as everyone seemed to come under suspicion. Despite the abundance of possible German suspects, Cobb's attention soon focused on two prominent German consuls: Frederick Rueter in Juárez, and Ernest H. Goeldner in Chihuahua. Investigation of their activities would center on propaganda and relations with the Mexican government, particularly Murguía. A new situation required different sources of information and Cobb recruited a number of new agents to address his two primary concerns. Two of them deserve particular attention.[59] The first, Mr. Anton Nesgaard, subsequently identified in correspondence simply as Mr. N., would initially report any German activity he observed.[60] Ultimately, he would concentrate on Goeldner and special activities in Chihuahua. As background, Cobb identified Nesgaard as:

> a Norwegian by birth, but a naturalized American citizen, who has resided for a number of years in the city of Chihuahua, and who has remained there up to this week throughout the revolutionary period. Mr. Nesgaard is vouched for by Americans who have known him in Chihuahua for years, and his statements are accepted without qualification as true and correct.[61]

The second agent, Norman Galentine, would report primarily on Rueter in Juárez. Galentine would remain particularly obscure in future traffic, identified only as "my party" or "Mr. _____ ," and his qualifications consisted of being "an old personally [sic] friend of German Consul Rueter . . . having lived near each other near Santa Rosalia, Mexico, for many years."[62] At least one commentator would view Cobb's work in this area and with these agents as "particularly successful."[63]

Mr. _____ provided remarkable insight into Rueter's operations in some twenty reports from August until December 1917. Early information covered relations between the German community and Murguía, while subsequent reports addressed propaganda activities. In this latter regard, Rueter's communications system gained intense scrutiny. Examination of telegraphic communications with Chihuahua, despite a monetary offer to a Mexican telegrapher, proved a dead end as German security concerns apparently prompted the use of wireless on this link to avoid suspect telegraphers.[64] Based on the changed manner in which Rueter "bradded" his papers, Cobb confirmed a connection "between agencies in Spain and German officials in Mexico . . . suggestive of their mode of operations."[65] A possible El Paso communications link resulted from the discovery that Rueter used an alias, Redolfo Uranga, to receive mail. Cobb indicated how he handled this information with caution.

> I am going to ask them [the local Justice agent and the El
> Paso Postmaster] to steam letters open for inspection, but, except
> in cases where the same should not be stopped because of their
> contents, not to stop transmission of such correspondence. My
> reasons are two fold: First, so as not to disclose my source of
> information, and second, so as not to destroy this new means of
> looking for things of importance.[66]

Cobb's plan for handling a new and sensitive source appears very
reasonable and professional. Nonetheless, like the telegraph lead,
this may not have resulted in information, as no reports based on
intercepted mail appear.[67]

Nesgaard served Cobb in a less insightful but equally important manner. He made repeated trips to Chihuahua at Cobb's
direction. Early trips resulted in a long list of German nationals
and their activity.[68] The most important development from this
general survey identified Otto Francis Zeschitz, "an Austrian,
who under the name of Garrison, served in our army, in Hawaii,
and elsewhere, . . . now working on maps for the German Consul."[69] Zeschitz made "particular inquiry about mountain passes,
water holes, etc. (information of a military nature), in the territory
covered by the Punitive Expedition, and in the section east of the
Central Railroad, between Chihuahua and Ojinaga."[70] In a follow-up report, Nesgaard provided additional details on both the
map and Zeschitz after an interview with the mapmaker, but
found him "so adroit and cautious . . . it [is] impossible to procure
either of the maps or prints from the same."[71] A final report on
Zeschitz anticlimactically indicated his commission in the Carranza military and continuing organizational activities for the foreign community and the Industrial Workers of the World.[72] Nesgaard's most important service came in detailed reporting on a
wireless station under construction in Chihuahua. Its importance
even required, at Cobb's direction, residence near the site.[73]

Reporting on the wireless tower started in February 1917 with
announcement of its planned construction in Chihuahua.[74]
Although originally assembled in Juárez by Villa, possible war

with the United States after the Columbus raid necessitated relocation of the large facility to Chihuahua. Its size reportedly interfered with smaller U.S. Army systems in El Paso.[75] Nesgaard's report seemed to confirm earlier suspicions of association of the wireless tower with the Germans via a wire connection from an old Chihuahua wireless station's operating room "across Second Street to a Mexican adobe building adjoining the Nordwald store."[76] Within two weeks of his original observations, Nesgaard confirmed his report with four photographs.[77] Cobb provided these photographs to Washington with detailed descriptions of their contents. On October 15, 1917, Cobb provided another set of Nesgaard photographs to Washington of the new 260-foot wireless tower.[78] In descriptive comments, Cobb included names and addresses of workers and others associated with the construction, further indicating a German connection. The old wireless, able to reach Torreón, adequately served German purposes, as indicated in comments regarding the timeliness of German reports.

> Another party, who is entirely reliable, informs me that the Germans frequently have news in Chihuahua of European happenings in advance of the receipt of the same news in the United States. He was particularly impressed, he says, with the fact that the fall of Riga [September 3, 1917] was announced by the Germans in Chihuahua three days before it was confirmed in American papers.[79]

Despite Cobb's efforts, the new wireless began operations on December 31, 1917.

While Nesgaard's and Galentine's operations provide more detail on intelligence operations, Cobb's greatest concern, based on number of messages, emotional content, and future plans, focused on German relations with Murguía and propaganda in Mexico. As already noted, Cobb held Murguía in little regard. Perhaps as an expression of disapproval, Cobb reported Murguía's transfer on several occasions, but in each instance later retracted his report. In Galentine's first report, he indicated strong connections between

Goeldner and Murguía and their participation in a picnic and parties in Juárez, along with several other German dignitaries, "at the expense of the German Consul Goeldner."[80] Cobb, while invited, refused to attend and subtly warned Mexican officials of repercussions.[81] Success with this measure dampened future public association between Murguía and the German community, but Cobb effectively used the incident to focus suspicion on Murguía's leanings and the level of German influence. Maintaining some objectivity in his view of Murguía, Cobb also reported a differing position.

> Mr Harrison [Cobb's British source near Parral] talked with him [Murguía] about the reports he was pro-German, and tried to impress on him that the Allies were certain to whip the Germans. In reply to this, Murguía made the evasive statement that he was no more pro-German than pro-Ally, that he was pro Mexican.[82]

Cobb seems eventually to have accepted this position and eased his apprehension over Murguía.

Propaganda proved an illusive target. In part, Cobb's difficulty with it may have come from his definition of the term. Any negative image of the United States, whether indigenous or foreign in origin, became propaganda. One editorial, roughly translated by agent H. J. Barron, from the Chihuahua *Heraldo del Norte* of June 6, can serve to fully illustrate the problem.

Yankees and Mexicans

Mexico does not need nor want the United States' educational influence and propaganda based on avowed intention of so called Mexico Corporation [*sic*] Society, Paul Kennedy to inaugurate an educational propaganda in Mexico.

How could we Mexicans expect or receive education from a race which regards no race other than those strictly white as human beings?

Why do we want educational aid from a materialistic, dollar greedy Yankeeland? We are a race of ideals, while Yankees are a race of dollar hunters, etc. Look back over our glorious history for proof.

The United States, defeated in its armed efforts to acquire Mexico, she now resorts to educational and political means of absorbing Mexico—knowing what a nervous and proud race Mexicans, etc.

With Veracruz and Pershing expedition availing naught, now come "educational" invaders.

Mexico does not want Yankee soldiers, dollars or political missionaries to teach its citizens. If we want culture, it is not North America to which we look—the Old World race from which we sprung is plenty good enough.[83]

Cobb found this thinking objectionable enough to send a copy to the Mexican Division of the State Department and under separate cover a second copy directly to the secretary of state. The message, not its source, defined the editorial as propaganda.

Some anti-American sentiment did originate from German sources. Cobb repeatedly provided details of German propaganda methods but efforts to destroy their apparatus proved futile. In his most spectacular coup, Cobb provided, direct from Rueter's desk, an extensive list of propaganda material.[84] He forwarded several copies to Washington and offered to obtain the entire set.[85] Information from an American serving in the Mexican customs office linked German propaganda and a contact in the United States.[86] Apparently on his own initiative, Cobb exercised direct coordination with the War Trade Board in Washington to break this link. These and other attempts failed to impair propaganda operations. Still concerned, Cobb traveled to Washington in early November to:

> submit to the Department, for consideration, plans by which we can not only eliminate German merchants and German propaganda in newspapers, picture shows, etc., but also discreetly, cautiously and effectively supersede them with American merchants and American propaganda in newspapers, picture shows, etc. It can be done.[87]

Reflecting his innovation with regard to ammunition, Cobb previously had proposed establishment and covert support of a pro-American paper in Chihuahua.[88] While no positive results on this suggestion appear, the trip to Washington deserves attention from other perspectives and for other accomplishments.

In conjunction with his trip, Cobb had his status as an intelligence agent confirmed in two ways. First, on September 18 he received an appointment as a special agent of the Department of State for matters along the Mexican border.[89] This included a nominal salary of unknown amount.[90] He would occupy this billet for approximately a year, but did not perform as an active agent. Additionally, he made contact with Colonel Ralph H. Van Deman, chief of the Military Intelligence Section, Department of War. Van Deman knew of Cobb based on the reports he had received from the State Department.[91] One item from Cobb, notable in the Military Intelligence files but absent from State Department files, concerns a recommendation "that a prohibited zone be established along the border, into which no transient Germans should be permitted to enter."[92] Implementation required checkpoints distant from the border to control access. Finally, based on this contact, Cobb advised Van Deman that Galentine's son, Norman Jr., had enlisted in the army and received an assignment as first sergeant, Company A, 3rd Balloon Squadron, and he recommended him for intelligence service.[93]

This trip also proved remarkable for several other reasons. First, Cobb's network in El Paso continued to report both directly to Washington over the signatures of his subordinates in the customs office and directly to him in Washington. This certainly indicates a disciplined and directed organization. Notably, none of his agent network reported through the customs office during this period. Second, Cobb's reports while in Washington originate under the letterhead of the War Trade Board. He had exercised some minor coordination with this organization over the past several months but his use of their facilities indicated a more active role in intelligence activities in Mexico. Finally, his return from this trip marked a significant change in his reporting procedures and practices. His message volume dropped sharply. From a strong involvement in border operations, he became uncharacteristically reticent in reporting events. In April 1918 he stopped sending reports to Washington and submitted his resignation from customs. His subordinates in El Paso customs continued reporting from severely diminished assets for a few months, then ceased.[94]

Concern with Germany rather than Mexico alone had brought Cobb into the ranks of professional agents along the border. He deftly supervised a string of carefully selected agents who gathered an impressive amount of information. Their depth of penetration into targeted German operations and technical means of collection contrast sharply with Cobb's previous use of a more haphazard and circumstantial approach to soliciting information. Although he showed an interest in the more formal intelligence structures established in Washington, he displayed surprisingly little coordination with local intelligence agencies. Since he had achieved a high level of success as an intelligence agent along the border and openings with powerful men in Washington, his departure from activities that added to his official position appears as a stunning move. Despite his aptitude for intelligence, Cobb always remained a politician, and, while one avenue to power and influence had ended, another door had opened.

CHAPTER FIVE

Moving Out, Up, and On

RESIGNATION FROM CUSTOMS closed Cobb's direct and significant involvement in border intelligence operations, but neither his life nor political ambitions had ended. Pursuits after his tenure as collector show his orientation toward politics, public service, and to a lesser extent, Mexico and intelligence. Undoubtedly reflecting previous gestation, an article in the *El Paso Herald* of March 29, 1918, indicated a groundswell of support for Cobb as the Democratic nominee in the party primary for the newly established Texas 16th Congressional District.[1] Support from women activists and other political stalwarts, such as Dan M. Jackson, found rapid political opposition. On April 1, 1918, Claude B. Hudspeth, an old political opponent, announced formation of a committee of prominent supporters "to plan a line of action to combat the efforts of numerous friends of Zach Lamar Cobb, customs collector, to have him enter the race against Mr. Hudspeth."[2] Among Hudspeth's supporters stood Tom Lea, the former mayor; Joseph

Nealon, Cobb's former law partner; and W. W. Turney, a former state senator. While Hudspeth invited him to meet in debate, Cobb, not yet a candidate, placed duty above politics and opened a Liberty Bond campaign in Albuquerque "upon invitation of [the] Dallas [Federal] Reserve Bank."[3] Heeding the political opportunity, on April 4 Cobb submitted his resignation to Secretary of the Treasury William MacAdoo and entered the race for Congress.[4]

He presented a viable platform supporting women's suffrage, prohibition, and the president's war efforts. The slogan and campaign platform, "One Hundred Per Cent Americanism; Stand by the President; Help whip the Kaiser," adorned his campaign literature.[5] Strangely, with regard to his position for running, he stated:

> That I am not seeking election to Congress for the sake of office or for the the money there may be in it, is shown by the fact that the office from which I have just resigned pays nearly as much as does the office of Congressman, without the expense attached to life in Washington.[6]

While nominally running on his record, which of course he viewed as superior to his opponent's, Cobb provided a characterization of his service as collector just prior to his resignation.

> If I resign my office tonight, I shall leave the most delightful position in this section. I have enjoyed the affection of every employee and of the president and those at Washington with whom I had to deal. Office is a thing of honor, but there are greater things than mere office. Wilson is known as president today, but when historians write of this period, he will be known as the foremost American of his time.[7]

Beyond mere campaign rhetoric, these selections discreetly outline the issues and vulnerabilities of the campaign. Cobb would run on his record as a Wilson man, supporting suffrage and prohibition. In the politics of the time, he stood as an outsider from the regular party machine that supported Hudspeth. Positions and personalities bore striking similarity to the 1912 Texas Democratic Party

Convention in Houston when Cobb gained a seat as a delegate against the machine.

Little immediate campaigning took place. Nonetheless, Cobb and Hudspeth found early support with the two El Paso newspapers, the *Herald* and *Morning Times*, respectively. Each candidate appeared to concentrate on building organization and funds for the period immediately prior to the July 27 primary election. Accordingly, in early July, the fighting and the mudslinging really started.

Overall, Hudspeth seemed to have had the better end of the execution of his political tactics. He attacked Cobb in a number of small banner headlines in the *El Paso Morning Times*.

Is it possible for a Congressional candidate Who Owns no Liberty Bonds to be 100% American?

If Zach Cobb could raise a 7,501.54 Campaign Fund Why couldn't he Raise the Money to OWN a few Liberty Bonds?

Mr. Cobb Claims the support of Secretary Lansing. Has Mr. Lansing been Informed About the Cobb Liberty Loan Record?

The Kaiser Needs no better friends in the United States than the 5,000 a Year Man Who owns no Liberty Bonds.[8]

Other Hudspeth statements outlined Cobb's earlier failed political attempts and suggested his delivery of "a speech against prohibition with his arms around a negro woman."[9] Charges of owed back taxes on 1,400 acres and a city lot shared a late-breaking pre-election newspaper article.[10] Other than a minor challenge to Cobb's role in Huerta's arrest, however, Hudspeth never attacked Cobb's record or performance as collector.[11]

Cobb had minor success against these accusations. He declared the antiprohibition speech scenario false and simply ignored the challenge to his role in the Huerta arrest. In probable anticipation of the attack, the *El Paso Herald* had earlier noted Cobb's bond

ZACH LAMAR COBB

OF EL PASO, TEXAS

Zach Lamar Cobb

CANDIDATE FOR CONGRESS

FROM THE 16TH DISTRICT

PLATFORM:

100 Per Cent Americanism; Stand by the President; Help Whip the Kaiser; For Prohibition; For Woman Suffrage.

Published by the
COBB CAMPAIGN COMMITTEE,
Suite 616 Caples Building, El Paso, Texas.
Phones 2731 and 2510.

Front panel of a campaign trifold flyer used during Cobb's unsuccessful bid for the Democratic party nomination in 1916. (Courtesy of Dallas Historical Society.)

purchases but still failed to make an adequate response against charges involving lack of a Liberty Bond. Early in the campaign, Cobb had outlined his financial status.

> I am a poor man, without a dollar on earth. Investments that I made before I took my present office proved unfortunate and by them I was left in a debt I was unable to pay. Now, one's homestead is exempt under the law of Texas, but under the law of God no man claims exemption, and so I and my wife left our homestead and went into a rented apartment. I had been told that if I made this race opponents would say I had failed to pay my debts. I ask them to say also that in my four years as customs collector, when speculation ran rife on the border, I turned my back to all private business.[12]

Despite apparent ammunition, Cobb never successfully responded to smears involving his bond purchase and financial record. In general, he ran a clean public campaign, countering only with some mud regarding Hudspeth's birth, contrary to claims, outside Texas. Behind the scenes, however, Cobb tried to call in political favors to ensure his election.

Contacting a principal supporter, highly regarded Texas politician Thomas B. Love, then serving as assistant secretary of the treasury, Cobb pleaded for specific backroom support. Interestingly, at Love's request, each treated their correspondence "as absolutely confidential."[13] High on Cobb's list of actions stood the endorsement of the prohibition organization "Home and State." In June, a month after his request, he distributed a flyer indicating support from "Home and State" and the chairman of the Texas Suffrage Association. Cobb believed that suffrage and prohibition, generally viewed as dead issues, possessed potential.

> Prohibition and Woman Suffrage will be live issues in this state until both are made part of the constitution. As the situation now is, either or both may be assailed in court or may be repealed at the next or some succeeding session of the legislature.[14]

Beyond any personal philosophical commitment, that both issues could attract votes undoubtedly played a role in Cobb's support for these particular views.

Two days after his initial request to Love, Cobb discreetly suggested pressure on a senior Hudspeth supporter.

> Senator W. W. Turney, who, as you know, was recently appointed as one of the El Paso directors of the branch bank of the Federal Reserve of Dallas, is the most active and the most influential man who is supporting Hudspeth against me.
>
> There isn't a man on the Federal Reserve Board who doesn't know my service to this government. . . . Isn't it inconsistent for Senator Turney, whose prestige has been increased by government appointment, to be actively endeavoring to defeat the administration man in this race?[15]

Since Turney served on the Dallas Federal Reserve Board, which invited Cobb to launch the Albuquerque Liberty Bond drive, and considering the volatility of the bond issue for Cobb, circumstances led to obvious speculation. Although no direct evidence exists, dirty politics in the Hudspeth organization may have started earlier than the July headlines.

In the same letter, Cobb identified an additional grievance against Turney and his sensitivity to press criticism.

> The *El Paso Times* is nominally owned here, but it is mortgaged to New York, and is recognized as a Phelps-Dodge paper. Mr. H. J. Simmons, who is now running the *Times*, told me, before I entered the race, that they wouldn't oppose me. Under the influence of Turney, they are opposing me, though they are not doing so as aggressively as they probably will. A word from Cleveland Dodge, to Mr. Simmons, about my service to the administration, and the value that I would be to the administration in Washington, would shut the *Times* up and leave Hudspeth without formidable newspaper support in this section.[16]

Events indicate that pressure, if any materialized, failed to turn either Turney or the paper to Cobb's favor.

Love did take at least one additional action in Cobb's support. On July 15, Love wrote to J. P. Tumulty, the president's secretary, requesting the president's endorsement.

> If a note could be sent Cobb, referring to his services to the administration and expressing the hope that he will be nominated, and, in view of the shortness of time, he could be advised of the purport of the note by wire, it would undoubtedly be very effective in preventing another McLemore being sent to represent the El Paso District in the next House of Representatives.[17]

Unfortunately, reflecting the president's impartial and uninvolved attitude designed to avoid party fratricide, no response came.[18] In the face of the regular party machine, lack of a presidential endorsement, and an ineffective response to campaign charges, Cobb lost the election.

Reaction to the loss reflects aspects of spirit and bitterness, along with an element of racism, in Cobb.

> It was some race! . . . I came to the El Paso line with about a three hundred majority.
>
> El Paso County gave me a clear majority of its white American vote. My home precinct went for me, two to one. Having a majority in the outside counties, and a majority of the white people here, the election was taken away from us at the cost of about $30,000, by the purchasable, the negro and illiterate Mexican, vote. I have won a victory in defeat.[19]

Cobb's privately voiced racial sentiment and analysis also reflects public expressions. On July 26, the day before the election, the *El Paso Morning Times* had carried an article announcing "Colored women endorse candidates on Regular Democratic Ticket."[20] A later editorial in the *El Paso Herald* more closely reflected Cobb's statement.

The analysis of the vote was interesting. Cobb carried the majority of the American polling places, while Hudspeth received the majorities in all the precincts where the negro and Mexican vote was cast.[21]

Cobb, while not as vehement as many, failed to rise above the pervasive racism of his community.

Defeat meant a need for new position to provide income. Cobb expressed his still burning ambition and aspirations to Love.

The general expectation is that I will be reappointed Collector of Customs. I do not want it. I want something bigger, although I do not care whether it is bigger in title or merely bigger in the spirit with which I would accept any assignment in which I can render service to help win this war.[22]

Cobb, in compliance with his more spiritual wishes, soon received an assignment to the War Trade Board in Washington as the country adviser for Mexico.[23]

Records for the War Trade Board do not clearly indicate Cobb's period of service. Based on correspondence in their records, he was in Washington from December 1918 until early May 1919. Perfectly suited to his apparent duties, he established and tracked enforcement of export regulations applied to Mexico. He also remained in the intelligence loop between State and War, both because of his billet and his continued responsibilities as a State Department special agent.[24] Munitions, wireless apparatus, newsprint, and films headed the list of special material subject to export control and Cobb's official comment.

Seemingly innocuous bureaucratic duties at the War Trade Board still possessed undertones of intelligence activities. Among his few positive actions, Cobb signed off on a policy relaxing control over newsprint in February 1919. Interestingly, the War Trade Board exercised control over newsprint in part as a result of a problem Cobb had identified and tentatively resolved while still serving as collector. In March 1918, he had reported Consul Goeldner's possible employment as a reporter for *El Correo* in Chihuahua City. Dependent "on paper issued day by day," if it had published any material favorable to Germany, Cobb would have stopped the export of newsprint.[25] Within the War Trade Board, Cobb may have worked with the chairman's assistant, Captain J. Foster Dulles, on this and other matters. Dulles wrote memoranda directing quiet control of the export of newsprint. He also received a request from Colonel Van Deman to restrict shipment of wireless apparatus to Mexico to enable continued valuable intelligence exploitation of a "40 kilometer [wire] gap between Ojinaga and the nearest inland station."[26]

Departure from the War Trade Board marked Cobb's return to El Paso. With his apparent resignation from duties as a State Department special agent in August 1919, he became totally dependent on a private legal practice for income.[27] Separation from intelligence seemed complete. An offer to serve as an informal agent of the Military Intelligence Division in May 1920 apparently went unanswered.[28] As an attorney, Cobb participated in the establishment of the El Paso Bar Association and continued an interest in Mexican affairs.[29] Mexico's renewed contest for power, this time between Obregón and Carranza, provided a new opportunity for Cobb.

In May 1920, after desultory coordination with the State Department, Cobb accepted a retainer from Roberto Pesqueira to act as a legal counsel.[30] Pesqueira served as financial agent for the new movement supporting Obregón and acted for Adolfo de la Huerta, governor of Sonora and temporary executive of the new state government. In this capacity, Cobb wrote to the new secretary of state, Bainbridge Colby. After offering personnel advice regarding Polk and Boaz Long, a long-time departmental adviser on Latin American affairs, Cobb suggested a course of action on Mexican affairs.

> You can solve the Mexican problem, so as to establish a government there without military intervention and so as to relieve the Administration of this particular burden in the approaching Presidential campaign, provided you get out from under the

abominable departmental system of choking every good idea to death with innumerable memoranda, referred to everybody and acted upon by nobody. . . . If you will permit me to do so, I will bring well selected, accredited representatives of the de facto government to Washington to deal with you directly, to lay their cards on the table and, with your counsel, to formulate a program of what Mexico must do to gain the help of our government, first, for recognition as a de facto government; second, for the concurrent settlement of the oil disputes, the rehabilitation of the railroads, and re-financing of the government; and lastly, for a full recognition.[31] (Underlined in file copy.)

Despite an additional message indicating influence with Obregón and the oil interests, internal memos indicate that State declined Cobb's offer because:

Too many cooks *now*, as formerly, may spoil the broth. The new regime is apparently employing too many American attorneys, each insisting that he holds the destinies of our southern neighbor in his hand's palm. . . . negotiations with the new regime, when begun, will be conducted through regular diplomatic channels.[32] (Italic penciled into original. Underlining in original typed memo.)

Cobb may have identified the problem of killing good ideas in the State Department but his solution remained untenable.

Despite the potential opportunity for success with the new government as a client, Cobb's fortune had taken a slowly descending path. After failure to initiate or participate in talks between the two governments, he performed little of immediate consequence for Mexico. He sought and received clarification of the possible landing of U.S. Marines there, made an inquiry with the State Department on the availability of Carranza funds in United States banks, and kept Washington apprised of improvements in the new government's position.[33] His apparent failure to elicit positive results and the new government's quick consolidation of power after the death of Carranza on May 20 provide an explanation for the absence of additional actions on their behalf. Further, a Mexican government concentrating on consolidation of power and a Wilson administration hampered with elections for a new president and the impact of the Senator Albert B. Fall Investigation into U.S.-Mexican policy resulted in diplomatic deadlock. Not until April 1921, with a new Republican administration under Warren G. Harding, would Cobb return to Mexican affairs at the national level.

Apparently acting as a citizen with a private legal practice and without obvious ties to the Obregón government, inaugurated in late 1920, Cobb submitted an unusual suggestion to Washington. Writing to Henry P. Fletcher, formerly ambassador to Mexico and now serving as undersecretary of state, Cobb resurrected a proposal they had discussed two years earlier.

> The key to peaceful solution of our problems with Mexico is in the negotiation of a reciprocity treaty, to maintain and extend American commerce in Mexico, and to dispose of all annoying pending questions. . . . In my opinion, the time is now opportune to negotiate such an agreement with Mexico. I hope that our friend [George T.] Summerlin [the U.S. chargé d'affaires in Mexico City], who I see from the papers is on his way to Washington, will concur in this view.[34]

Fletcher and Summerlin discussed the letter and, at a private meeting in late May, Summerlin left a copy of a "proposed treaty of amity and commerce" with Obregón.[35] Unfortunately for Cobb, continuing impasse over oil exploitation and lack of recognition prohibited Mexican-U.S. negotiations over such a proposal at the time.[36]

Following this marginal success, Cobb later made two additional efforts which deserve notice. In February 1922 he shared a platform with Luís Montes de Oca, Mexican consul general in El Paso, and addressed the El Paso Branch of the Tri-State Association of Credit Men, a local chapter of a national trade organization. Published as a separate pamphlet, the two speeches and accompanying resolutions of the association urged recognition of Mexico and increased commercial ties. Cobb's speech, titled "Our Commercial

Relations with Mexico—The President Alone Can Break This Deadlock," reached the State Department from the U.S. consul in Juárez and President Harding from the governor of Arizona.[37]

In May 1922, as the second action of note, Cobb wrote Leland Harrison, a former intelligence associate at State and now assistant secretary of state, outlining a recent trip to Mexico City. Prefaced with mention of a personal conversation with Obregón and use of Pesqueira's private car, Cobb provided a three-page presentation of his observations, assessments, and recommendations. Harrison, after necessarily explaining Cobb's background, passed on one paragraph to Secretary of State Charles E. Hughes, who in turn passed selections from Cobb's letter to Harding. While not necessarily the most revealing paragraphs, after identifying Cobb, the material deemed of interest to the president read:

> The average politician of Mexico is a closer observer of European affairs than are the people of our own country. They watch every twist and turn in Europe. They are familiar with Russia and her policies of confiscation. They are watching the Genoa Conference to see just how far Russia can get away with it. If the great nations indulge Russia, you may expect a reflection of Russia's course in the attitude of Mexican politicians. If civilization stands firm against Russia, you may expect a discontinuance of confiscation in Mexico.

After speaking in complimentary terms of General Obregón, he added:

> But I want to see the recognition permanent, and I believe that its permanency depends upon impressing the Mexican leader, and doing so as friends, with the proposition that civilization, and particularly the United States, cannot recognize the right of any government to confiscate property.[38]

Cobb may not have known of the forwarding of his letter to the president, intended for the confidential use of Harrison and Hughes, as no return acknowledgement survives in the files.

These two items marked his last foray into diplomatic and Mexican affairs.

Sometime in late 1922, Cobb departed El Paso for Los Angeles, California, for unknown reasons.[39] His departure may have indicated a decline in business or a disgust with the rise of the Ku Klux Klan. An *El Paso Times* article of August 7, 1921, noted Cobb's participation in a public fight with a man evicted from his apartment as a result of actions Cobb filed on behalf of a client.[40] Public brawls rarely promote good business. More prominent in the decision to relocate may have been the temporary triumph of the El Paso Klan in 1921–1922. The local school board served as an important focus of initial Klan interest. In August 1921 Cobb energetically defended a client who had won a competitive bid to convert the schools to oil heat and supply oil against the school board's capricious withdrawal of the contract. While Cobb's pleas to the board on behalf of his client "intended no reflection upon the individuals composing the school board," it also noted their regrettable factional differences.[41] Shortly before his confrontation with the school board, that organization had terminated a school librarian over her religious affiliation. This stands as an early indicator of rising religious controversy on the board and in the community from the Klan.[42] The following year, having yet to announce his departure to California, Cobb publicly commented on the continuing dissension in his community.

> If we do not put a stop to this discord and the fight between people of different creeds and get together and come back to the old spirit that existed here, we might just as well move to some other community where such conditions do not exist.[43]

Cobb's departure serves as an opportunity to address an important aspect of his character.

Racism clearly surfaced in El Paso and permeated Texas and U.S. society in general at the time.[44] Cobb's comments on losing the election, as already noted, reflect a degree of racism. Isolated quotes from Cobb's messages and letters have in several contemporary books created an inaccurate impression of his racial attitudes. Despite reflecting the attitudes of the day, Cobb possessed an open mind and a sense of compassion. Many small and numerous already noted incidents indicate this side of Cobb. His treatment of Mrs. Villa in her flight from Mexico, his encouragement of the Red Cross in Juárez, condemnation of food export from Mexico while its citizens starved, and his pride in contacts throughout the community all reflect an unbiased character. Hints of community fear seep into his messages in times of crisis but, in general, his reporting lacks racial overtones, innuendo, or content.[45] Racism may have competed with greener political opportunities in motivating Cobb's move from El Paso.

In California, he joined the law firm of William MacAdoo for a period of time and may have participated in MacAdoo's unsuccessful campaign for the Republican presidential nomination in 1923. Cobb later established his own apparently very successful law office in downtown Los Angeles and remained active in local and national politics.[46] Although a Democrat, he maintained a politically independent mind. During the 1940 California Democratic primary he served as cochairman of the John Nance Garner for President Committee. Later, with Garner's failure, he split his support between the Republican Wendell Willkie and Democratic congressional candidates. Speaking before the California Democratic Luncheon Club on the subject, "Wanted, a United Nation," Cobb paid public contrition for opposing Franklin Roosevelt's third term. Grateful Democrats had the speech entered into the California State Senate Journal. In 1942, Cobb announced early support for nonpartisan gubernatorial candidate Earl Warren.[47] Cobb did not forget old friends. He maintained intermittent communications with General Pershing, discussing old friends such as Lawton Collins and Don Juan Brittingham, a source of information along the border and British Consul O'Hea's employer in Torreón. Pershing, in Washington, went so far as to take an interest in Brittingham's son, convalescing at Walter Reed Hospital in 1942.[48]

Remembering friends who had provided information and support during his service on the border appears as Cobb's last involvement in intelligence. Nine years later, on Thursday, December 20, 1951, Cobb died at home after a one-day illness.[49] He had earned a small place in the history of the border and intelligence as the collector of customs.

His service marked something of a transition in U.S. intelligence. During this period requirements for accurate information, starting with a confusing and perplexing situation in Mexico, outstripped traditional diplomacy and amateur espionage. Professional and disciplined agents, sent to elicit specific information or take directed action, evolved into an intelligence organization designed to satisfy government requirements. Cobb straddled the boundary between amateur and professional.

Originally involved as a means to further his influence and provide service to his party and benefactors, Cobb found himself in a position to fill a void on the border. Evolving from a mere relay in a communications link, he adapted skills acquired from his legal training, political activities, and family traditions to the requirements of intelligence. Possessed of an outgoing and ingratiating personality, with contacts across the border and up and down the social ladder, Cobb could elicit information and seemingly innocuous data from old friends and casual acquaintances with deceptive ease. Equally, his personal honesty gained and retained people's confidence. Like a good attorney, he recognized the need to confirm information, rarely accepting facts without independent corroboration, and generally separated facts from rumor and personal opinion in his reports. His first hallmark on the road to professional conduct came in defining the reliability of his sources as a means of evaluating their information. Cobb could weigh evidence, determine a degree of accuracy and reliability, and reach valid conclusions and observations. Additionally, he organized his material well. His ability to maintain continuity over time and present information clearly added to his impact in Washington and utility to historians.

His position as collector proved a mixed blessing. It provided a basis for authority and access to others in positions of influence, and brought potential sources to him. Conversely, shielded somewhat from State Department supervision and interference, he could expect little protection from Treasury direction in accomplishing supposed tasks from State. Additionally, he received little guidance in defining information of interest to Washington. As a result, he frequently overstepped his authority and reported overtly available information of interest to him and presumed to be of use in Washington. In the absence of guidance, nothing held special importance and everything was of equal value. Nonetheless, his omnivorous collecting and reporting and his development of covert sources alerted Washington to German influence in Mexico and impacted Washington's thinking in other areas as well. At the individual level, Cobb took full advantage of his position. He acted with independence as the situation demanded, as in the Huerta arrest and the coal embargo.

An important step in his professionalization came through contact with intelligence officers in the army and the Bureau of Investigation. He undoubtedly learned techniques and methods—basic tradecraft—through this association. The two most important lessons he applied were coordination and protecting sources. The first, in addition to an element of self-aggrandizement, may have motivated his effort at high-level coordination in 1915. Certainly, despite lapses, Cobb maintained close contact with other agencies in conducting his operations and obtaining information from them. His penchant for shielding his sources leaves many of them unknown even after a thorough examination of his reports. At the personal level, Cobb's ability or inability to speak and read Spanish remains unclear.

Professionalization and the end of amateur status came with authorization to employ and control agents. Cobb recruited able men who could travel at will without raising suspicion and who had contacts throughout the community, and he directed them, with little guidance from Washington, against specific targets.

Organizing a network capable of infiltrating a foreign community in a foreign land, gaining routine access to an opponent's desk, and photographing specific facilities remains a remarkable feat. Professionalization also increased the burden of competition with dedicated intelligence agencies and the required coordination and supervision from Washington. This, along with frustration in impacting events and an opportunity to gain further political power, influenced him to leave the intelligence field.

Despite his natural skill and ability and the impact his actions and reports had on the border and in Washington, Cobb remained at heart a politician. Against this backdrop, his overall contribution must be evaluated. Cobb's motivation came from his patriotism and party affiliation, rather than from business interests or anti-Villaism. He performed double duty for Washington during his service in El Paso: collector and intelligence agent. Unlike other border cities, El Paso was fortunate to have its own diplomat in residence.

ENDNOTES

INTRODUCTION

1. The various viewpoints are expressed in William Weber Johnson, *Heroic Mexico: The Narrative History of a Twentieth Century Revolution* (San Diego: Harcourt Brace Jovanovich, 1968); John Mason Hart, *Revolutionary Mexico: The Coming and Process of the Mexican Revolution* (Berkeley: University of California Press, 1987); and Friedrich Katz, *The Secret War in Mexico: Europe, the United States and the Mexican Revolution* (Chicago: University of Chicago Press, 1981).
2. See Rhodri Jeffreys-Jones, *American Espionage from Secret Service to CIA* (New York: Free Press, 1977); Charles D. Ameringer, *U.S. Foreign Intelligence: The Secret Side of American History* (Lexington, Conn.: D.C. Heath and Company, 1990); Allen Dulles, *The Craft of Intelligence* (New York: Harper and Row, 1963); Adda B. Bozeman, *Strategic Intelligence and Statecraft: Selected Essays* (Washington, D.C.: Brassey's, 1992); Christopher Andrew, *For the President's Eyes Only: Secret Intelligence and the American Presidency from Washington to Bush* (New York: HarperCollins Publishers, 1995); and George J. A. O'Toole, *Honorable Treachery: A History of U.S. Intelligence, Espionage and Covert Action from the American Revolution to the CIA* (New York: The Atlantic Monthly Press, 1991).
3. W. H. Timmons, *El Paso: A Borderlands History* (El Paso: Texas Western Press, 1990), 210.
4. Dulles, *The Craft of Intelligence*, 29.
5. Message of H. L. Wilson to Secretary of State, December 16, 1910, Records of the Department of State Relating to Internal Affairs of Mexico, 1910–1929, Department of State Decimal Files, Series 812.00/567. National Archives Microfilm Publication M274; General Records of the Department of State, Record Group 59. Hereafter cited as file number/document number.
6. Edward P. Haley, *Revolution and Intervention: The Diplomacy of Taft and Wilson with Mexico, 1910–1917* (Cambridge: Massachusetts Institute of Technology, 1970), 26.

119

7. Clarence Clendenen, *Blood on the Border: The United States Army and the Mexican Irregulars* (London: Macmillian Company, 1969), 144–145.
8. Haley, *Revolution and Intervention*, 20.
9. 812.00/390 message of November 19, 1910, H. L. Wilson to Secretary of State Philander Knox.
10. Dorothy Pierson Kerig, *Luther T. Ellsworth, U.S. Consul on the Border during the Mexican Revolution*, Southwestern Studies 47 (El Paso: Texas Western Press, 1975).
11. Graham H. Stuart, *American Diplomatic and Consular Practice* (New York: Appleton-Century-Crofts, 1936), Chapters 17 and 18 for background on the consul system.
12. 812.00/428 letter of November 19, 1910, Luther T. Ellsworth to Secretary of State.
13. Kerig, *Luther T. Ellsworth*, 38.
14. Kerig, *Luther T. Ellsworth*, 63.
15. Kendrick A. Clements, "Woodrow Wilson's Mexican Policy, 1913–1915," *Diplomatic History* 4 (Spring 1970): 114.
16. Larry D. Hill, *Emissaries to a Revolution: Woodrow Wilson's Executive Agents in Mexico* (Baton Rouge: Louisiana State University Press, 1973), 20.
17. Hill, *Emissaries*, 20. Internal quotes from E. David Cronon, ed., *The Cabinet Diaries of Josephus Daniels, 1913–1921* (Lincoln: University of Nebraska Press, 1963), 43.
18. Arthur S. Link et al., eds., *The Papers of Woodrow Wilson*, vol. 27 (Princeton: Princeton University Press, 1966–1993), 37, letter of July 17, 1913. Hereafter cited as Link, *PWW* (vol: page). Also see Clements, "Woodrow Wilson's Mexican Policy," 115.
19. John Milton Cooper, Jr., "'An Irony of Fate': Woodrow Wilson's Pre-World War I Diplomacy," *Diplomatic History*, 3 (Fall 1979): 435; and Link, *PWW* (28:268), letter of September 9, 1913, Wilson to Ellen Axson Wilson.
20. Hill, *Emissaries,* p. x.
21. Ibid., 130–135.
22. 812.00/10903 letter of February 10, 1914, Carothers to State; and Hill, *Emissaries,* 157.

CHAPTER 1

1. J. R. Lamar, "Howell Cobb," (in *Men of Mark in Georgia: Volume III: Covering the Period from 1733 to 1911*, William T. Northern, ed. (Atlanta: A.B. Caldwell, 1911), 3:566–81 at 566. For a complete genealogy of the Cobb family see John E. Cobb, *Cobb Chronicles* (Alexandria, Va.: Durant Publishers, 1985).
2. J. R. Lamar, "Howell Cobb," 567.

3. See Shelby Foote, *The Civil War: A Narrative* (New York: Random House, 1974), 3:643–44 for a description of the burning of Cherry Hill.

4. John Eddins Simpson, *Howell Cobb: The Politics of Ambition* (Chicago: Adams Press, 1973), 191.

5. Kermit L Hall, ed., *The Oxford Companion to the Supreme Court of the United States* (Oxford: Oxford University Press, 1992), 495.

6. Hall, *Supreme Court of the United States*, 493–94. Wilson and Lamar had in common a school teacher in Georgia, John T. Derry, a Confederate veteran, as the basis of their childhood friendship. Wilson left Georgia in 1873. Also see Josephus Daniels, *The Life of Woodrow Wilson 1856–1924* (Chicago: John C. Winston Company, 1924), 39. J. R. Lamar also wrote the short 1911 biography of Howell Cobb, Sr., noted above.

7. Cobb campaign flyer/handout of 1916, Dallas Historical Society, Love Papers, File A50.104, Correspondence 1918–1919, C. Correspondence Folder.

8. For Cobb's date of birth see 47523, Records of the Adjutant General, Record Group 94 (hereafter cited as AGO file number). Having clarified the family origins of Zach Lamar Cobb's name, an additional point remains. His name has suffered frequent misidentification at the hands of historians. Robert E. Quirk changed Cobb's first name to Zacharay in *The Mexican Revolution 1914–1915* (Bloomington: Indiana University Press, 1960), 44. O'Toole identified him as Zachary N. Cobb (*Honorable Treachery*, 234, 269). Hart used both Zach and Zack (*Revolutionary Mexico*, 270, 286–87), and Meyer employed Zachary (Michael C. Meyer, *Mexican Rebel: Pascual Orozco and the Mexican Revolution 1910–1915* [Lincoln: University of Nebraska Press, 1967], 119, 128, 129, 132). These misidentifications come as much from a paucity of previous work on Cobb as they do from Cobb's poor handwriting. Fortunately, most of his letters and messages were typed, but his signature remained occasionally illegible.

9. *El Paso Morning Times*, July 7, 1918. In an *El Paso Herald* article of November 2, 1972, describing the association between Bryan and El Paso, Nancy Hamilton described Cobb as Bryan's "long time friend."

10. For Sons of Confederate Veterans see *El Paso Herald*, March 19, 1902. For American Mining Convention see *El Paso Herald*, November 11 and 15, 1905.

11. *El Paso Herald*, September 29, 1909.

12. 812.00/10903 letter of February 10, 1914, Carothers to Bryan.

13. *El Paso Morning Times*, June 1, 1912.

14. Ibid.

15. See Arthur S. Link, "The Wilson Movement in Texas, 1910–1912," *Southwestern Historical Quarterly* 48 (October 1944): 167–85, for a description of pertinent Texas politics.

16. *El Paso Herald*, October 1, 1912.

17. Thomas B. Love Papers, Correspondence 1918–1919, C. Correspondence Folder; Cobb campaign flyer/handout for the states campaigned in; and *El Paso Herald*, October 3, 1912, for the land transaction. Cobb also retained his holdings in the Cobb Ranch, probably some 1,400 acres, within the Soccoro land tract on a portion of which he raised hogs.

18. *El Paso Herald*, January 14, 1913. John Mason Hart attributes Cobb's appointment to Colonel Edward Mandell House and John Henry Kirby (*Revolutionary Mexico*, 270, 286). However, Love deserves some of the credit as the leading Wilson man in Texas and Cobb's future political confidant. Additionally, Cobb's politics were decisively progressive and not as business oriented or as politically conservative as House's or Kirby's. Hart also identifies Cobb as an oil man in the same league as Duval West (*Revolutionary Mexico*, 287), a status which Cobb never attained.

19. Evan Anders, *Boss Rule in South Texas: The Progressive Era* (Austin: University of Texas Press, 1982), 200.

20. Ibid., 198.

21. *El Paso Herald*, January 14, 1913.

22. Anders, *Boss Rule*, 203.

23. *El Paso Herald*, September 24, 1913. Dr. Bush would gain some fame as the "Gringo Doctor."

24. For Cobb's salary see *Official Register, 1915* (Washington, D.C.: U.S. Government Printing Office, 1920), 245.

25. 812.00/23144 undated letter Letcher to State Department, 14. Since the letter provides a background to events, the specific date is irrelevant. Other material in the letter indicates a probable date of late 1915.

26. Ibid.

27. Ibid.

28. Ibid., 17 and 20.

29. S. L. A. Marshall, interview by Richard Estrada, transcript (University of Texas at El Paso: Institute of Oral History, July 1975), 21–23. Also see Richard Estrada, "Border Revolution: The Mexican Revolution in the Ciudad Juárez–El Paso Area, 1910-1915" (Master's thesis, University of Texas at El Paso, 1975), 129. Estrada also surmises that "Cobb's influence (however limited) with Wilson may have stemmed from a youthful acquaintance in Georgia, where Wilson lived for twelve years." As already noted, it was a Lamar relative who had the relationship with Wilson, not Zach Cobb.

30. Hill, *Emissaries*, 196–200.

31. Letter of June 27, 1914, Cobb to Gen. Hugh Lennox Scott, Hugh Lennox Scott Papers, Division of Manuscripts, Library of Congress, Box 15. For other Cobb endorsements of Carothers see Scott Papers Box 15, letter of May 2, 1914, Cobb to Scott; 812.00/12706 message of August 1, 1914, Cobb to Bryan, and /12934 message of August 7, 1914, Cobb to Bryan.

32. 812.00/11060 message of March 5, 1914, Cobb to Bryan.

33. 812.00/11074 message of March 6, 1914, Carothers to Bryan.
34. 812.00/11092 message of March 7, 1914, Cobb to Bryan.
35. 812.00/11230 letter of March 14, 1914, Cobb to Bryan, which includes a personal note, brought to Bryan's attention, of thanks from Terrazas to Cobb of March 12, 1914; and 812.00/12357 notation on a message of June 26, 1914, Carothers to Bryan.
36. Hill, *Emissaries*, 198.
37. Hill, *Emissaries*, 228.
38. 812.00/12706 message of August 1, 1914, Cobb to Bryan.
39. 812.00/12775b message of August 7, 1914, Bryan to Cobb, and /12934 message of August 7, 1914, Cobb to Bryan.
40. 812.00/15013 letter of August 20, 1914, Fuller to President Wilson.
41. 812.00/13517 message of August 21, 1914, Cobb to Bryan.
42. See 812.00/13128 letter of September 5, 1914, Cobb to Bryan for the suggestion, and /13119 message of September 7, 1914, Bryan to Fuller via the Brazilian Minister in Mexico City for implementation.
43. 812.2311/130 message of August 23, 1914, Cobb to Bryan.
44. 812.2311/130 message of August 24, 1914, Bryan to Cobb.
45. 812.00/27428 letter of August 29, 1914, Cobb to Bryan.
46. 812.2311/150 message of August 27, 1914, Cobb to Bryan for first two quotes, and 812.00/27428 letter of August 29, 1914, Cobb to Bryan for latter quote.
47. 812.2311/150 message of August 27, 1914, Cobb to Bryan.
48. 812.2311/153 message of August 26, 1914, Cobb to Bryan.
49. 812.2311/157 message of August 27, 1914, Carothers to Bryan.
50. See 812.00/13043 message of August 30, 1914, Cobb to Bryan, and /27429 message of August 31, 1914, Cobb to Bryan for the change of recommendation. For Pershing's rapidly changing orders see 812.2311/169 message of August 31, 1914, General Bliss to Pershing, and /165 message of September 1, 1914, Bryan to Cobb.
51. 812.00/13043 message of August 30, 1914, Cobb to Bryan.
52. 812.00/13065 message of September 1, 1914, Cobb to Bryan. Also see Hill, *Emissaries*, 236–38, for additional details. Hill presents the events as flowing much more smoothly.
53. 812.2311/159 message of August 27, 1914, Cobb to Bryan.
54. See 812.4066 for letter of January 12, El Paso Ministers to Bryan, message of January 27, Bryan to Cobb, and January 31, Cobb to Bryan (all 1915).
55. Scott Papers, Box 16, letter of September 21, 1914, and undated letter of July 1914, both Cobb to Scott.
56. See messages 812.00/12266, June 16, 1914; /122283, June 17, 1914; /12800, August 10, 1914; /12840, August 13, 1914; /13089, September 3, 1914; /15118, April 16, 1915; and /15099, May 31, 1915. All Cobb to Bryan.
57. 812.00/12387 message of July 1, 1914, Cobb to Bryan.

58. 812.00/13657 message of November 2, 1914, Cobb to Bryan.

59. 812.00/12914 message of August 18, 1914, Cobb to Bryan.

60. AGO 2159332 of April 28, 1914, Cobb to Tumulty, secretary to President Wilson. Coincidentally General Scott discussed volunteers with Cobb's brother, William McKinley Cobb, on April 23, 1914, Scott Papers, Box 15. The name William McKinley reflects the maiden name of Cobb's mother rather than a presidential connection. William worked in Room 223, House Office Building, Washington, D.C.

61. Scott Papers, Box 15, letter of May 17, 1914, Cootes to Scott.

62. Papers of General John J. Pershing, Manuscript Division, Library of Congress, Box 48, letter of May 13, 1914, Cobb to Pershing.

63. Pershing Papers, Box 372, Original Reports and Documents, File: Mexican Border 1914–1916, Folder 2, part 1, memorandum from the Provost Marshal dated June 2, 1915. The provost marshal was a second lieutenant in the 16th Infantry. His signature is illegible. The memorandum had no "To" line, but inclusion in the Pershing papers indicates Pershing as the recipient.

64. Scott Papers, Box 16, letter of July 16, 1914, Bliss to Scott.

65. 812.00/12559 letter of July 20, 1914, Secretary of War to Secretary of State.

66. 812.00/12725 U.S. Army, Southern Department weekly report no. 71, dated July 25, 1914, 3.

67. 812.00/12725 U.S. Army, Southern Department, weekly report no. 71, dated July 25, 1914, 6. Note the similarity to Bliss's terminology.

68. See 812.00/12887 weekly report of the Southern Department for August 8, 1914, and 812.113/3504 message of August 8, 1914, Cobb to Bryan respectively.

69. *El Paso Herald*, April 28, 1915.

70. 812.00/12741 letter of July 3, 1914, Cobb to Bryan, and letter of July 28, 1914, Bryan to Cobb.

71. 812.00/12706 message of August 1, 1914, Cobb to Bryan. Similar concern is expressed in /13128 letter of September 15, 1914, Cobb to Bryan.

72. See 812.00/12601 message of July 24, 1914, Cobb to Bryan for cattle transaction, and /13128 letter of September 5, 1914, Cobb to Bryan for quote. Also see Manuel A. Machado, Jr., *The North Mexican Cattle Industry, 1910–1975* (College Station: Texas A&M University Press, 1981), chap. 1, "An Industry Destroyed, 1910–1920," 7–28, for an excellent overview.

73. 812.00/13128 letter of September 9, 1914, Bryan to Cobb.

74. 812.00/14473 message of March 2, 1915, Cobb to Bryan.

75. See 812.00/15132 letter of April 27, 1915, Cobb to Bryan, and /15098 message of May 31, 1915, Carothers to Bryan via Cobb.

76. See 812.00/23114 undated letter, Letcher to Bryan, and /24271 letter of June 14, 1914, Cobb to Bryan for the bullet.

77. 812.00/15108 letter of April 15, 1915, Cobb to Bryan.

78. 812.00/15099 message of June 1, 1915, Cobb to Bryan.

79. See Hart, *Mexican Revolution*, 153, 294; Alan Knight, *The Mexican Revolution* (Cambridge: Cambridge University Press, 1986), 2:115, 169; and Thomas Benjamin and Mark Wasserman, *Provinces of the Revolution: Essays on Regional Mexican History, 1910–1929* (Albuquerque: University of New Mexico Press, 1990), 56. Benjamin and Wasserman cite Hart, Knight, and Robert E. Quirk (*The Mexican Revolution 1914–1915*, 53–54). Quirk contains no allegation against Cobb or U.S. Customs regarding coal.

80. 812.00/12219 message of June 12, 1914, Carothers to Bryan via Cobb.

81. 812.00/12370 message of June 29, 1914, Cobb to Bryan. Cobb probably based this information and assessment on a meeting with De La Garza that same day. See /12370 letter of June 29, 1914, Cobb to Bryan, for an account of the meeting.

82. 812.00/12470 message of July 11, 1914, Cobb's summary to Bryan of lengthy and subsequently mailed letter Carothers to Bryan. Also see /12468 for report of implementation of the agreement.

83. 812.00/12706 message of August 1, 1914, Cobb to Bryan.

84. See 812.00/27428 letter of August 29, 1914, Cobb to Bryan; /13065 message of September 1, 1914, Cobb to Bryan; and 812.2311/173, Pershing's report of September 14, 1914.

85. See 812.00/13984 of December 10, 1914, Secretary of the Treasury to Secretary of State, and /1400 December 12, 1914, Cobb to Bryan, for the trip to Washington.

86. See 812.00/13529, October 18, 1914; /13549, October 19, 1914; /13562, October 21, 1914; /13584, October 23, 1914; and /1316, October 28, 1914, for Cobb's administrative problems.

87. See Records of the Department of State, Purport Lists for the Department of State Decimal File, 119.251, Department of State–Consular Code–Red, 9–11, entries 311, 315, 319, 343, and 344. National Archives Microfilm Publication M973, roll 13; General Records of the Department of State, Record Group 59.

88. 812.00/15188 message of April 16, 1915, Cobb to Bryan.

89. 812.00/5105 letter of April 15, 1915, Cobb to Bryan.

90. See 812.00/14999 message of May 11, 1915, Cobb to Bryan.

91. 812.00/15155 message of June 7, 1915, Cobb to Bryan.

92. See 812.00/15132 letter of April 27, 1915, Cobb to Bryan, for first two sources, and /14983 message of May 7, 1915, Cobb to Bryan, regarding newspaper attitudes and reports.

93. 812.00/15132 letter of April 27, 1915, Cobb to Bryan.

94 See 812.00/15044 message of May 20, 1915, Cobb to Bryan, for Cobb's request and background on the incident, and /15191 letter of May 24, 1915, and June 8, 1915, State to Cobb, for Washington's action.

CHAPTER 2

1. See Knight, *Mexican Revolution*, 2:323–25, for a description of the battles.
2. *Foreign Relations of the United States, 1915* (Washington, D.C.: U.S. Government Printing Office, 1940), 694–95. Hereafter *FRUS, 1915.*
3. Haley in *Revolution and Intervention: The Diplomacy of Taft and Wilson with Mexico, 1910–1917* (Cambridge: Massachusetts Institute of Technology, 1970) states, "Only by a play on the term could Wilson be considered a counterrevolutionary. He made no attempt to 'counter' the Mexican revolution or to turn back the clock in the sense one normally understands as counterrevolutionary. Rather, he attempted prematurely to 'sublimate' the revolutionary struggle into constitutional channels" (186).
4. For details on the Huerta-German connection see Barbara Tuchman, *The Zimmermann Telegram* (New York: Viking Press, 1958; reprint, New York: Ballantine Books, 1985), chap. 6, 66–87; Michael C. Meyer, "The Mexican-German Conspiracy of 1915," *The Americas* 23 (1967): 76–89; George J. Rausch, Jr., "The Exile and Death of Victoriano Huerta," *Hispanic American Historical Review* [*HAHR*] 42 (May 1962): 133–51, and Katz, *The Secret War in Mexico,* chap. 6, 203–49.
5. *El Paso Herald*, June 26, 1915.
6. 812.001/H87/20 message of June 26, 1915, Cobb to Bryan.
7. Ibid., Lansing to Cobb.
8. 812.001/H87/21 message of June 27, 1915, Cobb to State.
9. *El Paso Herald*, Monday, June 28, 1915. No reason for the concern of federal officers with diminished arrest authority on crossing state lines could be determined.
10. *El Paso Herald*, Monday, June 28, 1915.
11. This account comes from Cobb's reports and the two referenced El Paso papers, which sent reporters and took pictures. Other accounts of the Huerta arrest differ from this version in that they have Huerta alighting from the train, greeting Orozco in a waiting car, and Cobb or Marshal Bryant stepping out from behind some boxes or shrubbery in Newman, New Mexico, to make the arrest/invitation. See Tuchman, *Zimmermann Telegram*, 81; Meyer, "The Mexican-German Conspiracy of 1915," *The Americas*, 86; Rausch, "Exile and Death," *HAHR*, 139, and Don M. Coerver and Linda B. Hall, *Texas and the Mexican Revolution: A Study in State and National Border Policy 1910–1920* (San Antonio, Tex.: Trinity University Press, 1984), 113. These differences, while not substantive, appear to originate with the use of an inaccurate *New York Times* article of June 28, 1915 (intimated in Tuchman and referenced in Rausch), which reads: "The sun was just above the horizon when the train was flagged by United States troops and deputies, and General Huerta alighted. First to embrace him was tall Pascual Orozco, who had driven up in an automobile a few minutes before and had kept his

engine racing as if he would spirit the former provisional President across the river. As the two Generals who had opposed each other in the death struggle of the Orozco revolution at Bachimba embraced in the manner of the Mexican people, Deputy Marshal Edward Bryant stepped from behind a pumphouse and informed the Generals that he would be forced to detain them both and that he preferred to have them accompany him without the use of the troops in command of Colonel George H. Morgan."

12. *El Paso Morning Times*, Monday, June 28, 1915.

13. 812.001/H87/18 message of 11 a.m., June 27, 1915, Cobb to State. Lea had taken office on April 29, 1915, beating his opponent from the local political machine in the primary. The heaviest voting in the city's history had given Lea 4,218 votes to his opponent's 3,149. See *El Paso Herald*, February 17 and April 29, 1915.

14. *El Paso Herald*, Monday, June 28, 1915. This may not be mere publicity and exaggeration. George J. Rausch, Jr., states, "Had Huerta been able to reach Mexico in June, 1915, his chances of success would have been good. The forces which had originally opposed him had divided into rival factions, and civil war between Villa and Carranza followed. Less than two months earlier the Villa forces had been decisively defeated. Although they still held northern Mexico they were badly demoralized and large numbers would probably have deserted to Huerta, or to any other promising opponent of Carranza. In addition, remnants of the federal army would have undoubtedly joined his banner. . . . Perhaps most important of all, Huerta had been offered German financial support." ("The Exile and Death of Victoriano Huerta," 149.)

15. 812.001/H87/21 message of 9 a.m., June 27, 1915, Cobb to Lansing.

16. 812.001/H87/20 message of June 28, 1915, State to Cobb.

17. 812.001/H87/21 and /18 messages of June 27, 1915, State to President, who was vacationing at Windsor, Vermont. The first forwarded Cobb's initial 9 a.m. report (/21) and the second, at 11 a.m. (/18), covered Huerta's removal to Fort Bliss.

18. Rausch, "The Exile and Death of Victoriano Huerta," *HAHR*, 136–37, and O'Toole, *Honorable Treachery*, 240.

19. See 812.001/H87/27 message of July 1, 1915, Cobb to State, /30 message of July 2, 1915, Cobb to State, and 812.00/15445 message of July 14, 1915, Cobb to State, as examples of Cobb's concern with counterrevolutionary forces.

20. 812.001/H87/22 message of June 28, 1915, Cobb to State.

21. See endnote 17 above and 812.001/H87/34 message of July 3, 1915, Cobb to State, /37 message of July 5, 1915, Cobb to State, and /44 message of July 8, 1915, Cobb to State.

22. 812.00/15386 letter of June 30, 1915, Cobb to State.

23. 812.001/H87/44 message of July 9, 1915, Lansing to Cobb.

24. See Mark T. Gilderhus, *Diplomacy and Revolution* (Tucson: University of Arizona Press, 1977), 23.

25. Harris, Charles H. III and Louis R. Sadler, *The Border and the Revolution: Clandestine Activities of the Mexican Revolution 1910–1920,* 2nd ed. (Silver City, N. Mex.: High-Lonesome Books, 1990), 71. Timmons (*El Paso*, 219–20) relates that news of the plan contributed to racial hatred along the border and demands of additional troops for the city. Cobb contributed to State Department perceptions of the situation with the forwarding of a private report from a Hearst correspondent in Brownsville, Texas, in late September 1915. The reporter found the incident "neither an international trouble nor is it racial" but rather "a band of former federal and disgruntled Villistas" and "Huerta sympathizers" causing trouble along with "American citizens . . . kill[ing] off a number of Mexican voters of the stronger party." See 812.00/16289 message of September 26, 1915, Cobb to State, for the reporter's views.

26. See Gilderhus, *Diplomacy and Revolution*, 24, and Haley, *Revolution and Intervention*, 161.

27. Clements, "Woodrow Wilson's Mexican Policy, 1913–15," 135.

28. 812.48/2628 message of July 12, 1915, Cobb to State (Personal).

29. See 812.00/15431 message of July 13, 1915, Cobb to State, and 812.48/2677 letter of July 15, 1915, Cobb to Lansing for complaints. Villa promised to remove these very men to Carothers a few days later (see 812.00/15490 message of July 19, 1915, Carothers to State).

30. See 812.48/2628 message of July 12, 1915, 812.00/15457 message of July 15, 1915, and 812.00/15630 message of August 3, 1915, all Cobb to State.

31. 812.00/15445 message of July 14, 1915, Cobb to State.

32. Ibid., /15457 message of July 15, /15476 of July 17, /15489 of July 22, and /15545 and /15546 of July 26. All Cobb to State.

33. See 812.00/15721 message of August 10, 1915, Cobb to State, and /15719 message of August 11, 1915, Lansing to Scott. See Hill, *Emissaries,* 347–49, for a discussion of the Scott-Villa talks.

34. Machado, *The North Mexican Cattle Industry*, 16.

35. Ibid., 16–18, for views on Lansing's actions, and Gilderhus, *Diplomacy and Revolution*, 28.

36. Machado, *North Mexican Cattle Industry*, 17–18.

37. Hill, *Emissaries*, 347. Also see Gilderhus, *Diplomacy and Revolution*, 28, and *Foreign Relations of the United States, The Lansing Papers*, vol. 2 (Washington, D.C.: U.S. Government Printing Office, 1940), 545–48 for discussion and original correspondence between Wilson and Lansing on the abattoir and the support of Villa.

38. See Louis G. Khale, "Robert Lansing and the Recognition of Venustiano Carranza," *HAHR* 38 (August 1958): 353–72.

39. Naylor, Thomas H., "Massacre at San Pedro de la Cueva: The Significance of Pancho Villa's Disastrous Sonora Campaign," *Western Historical Quarterly* 8 (April 1977): 150. The article provides a comprehensive examination of Villa's Sonoran campaign.

40. For a discussion of the importance of the Port of El Paso to Villa, see Estrada, *Border Revolution*, 111–38, and Timmons, *El Paso*, 209–21.

41. 812.00/16503 message of October 16, 1915, Cobb to State.

42. Ibid.

43. 812.00/16559 message of October 22, 1915, Cobb to State.

44. 812.00/16612 message of October 27, 1915, Cobb to State.

45. 812.00/16559 message of October 22, 1915, Cobb to State. The same message reports profits to Villa of over twelve thousand dollars from the sale of sheep in the few previous days.

46. 812.00/16628 and /16564 messages of October 22, 1915, Cobb to State. A State note attached to /16564 reads, "Treasury has instructed Cobb not to take above matter up with State Department."

47. 812.00/16612 memorandum of October 28, 1915, Division of Mexican Affairs.

48. 812.00/16628 memorandum of October 23, 1915, Office of the Solicitor to the Division of Mexican Affairs, and /16612 letters of October 30, 1915, State to Treasury and Agriculture.

49. 812.00/16629 letter of October 22, 1915, Treasury to State.

50. 812.00/16612 message of November 1, 1915, State to Cobb for first quote regarding Lansing's USDA support to Cobb; same file letter of October 26, 1915, State to Cobb for second quote pertaining to State's railroad response; and 812.00/16630 message of October 23, 1915, Cobb to State, for Cobb's subservient but pleading response to State regarding Treasury instructions.

51. 812.00/16634 message of October 27, 1915, Cobb to State. Also see /16678 letter of November 1, 1915, Agencia Confidencial del Gobierno Constitucionalista de México to Lansing, which placed the number of railway cars involved at 208.

52. 812.00/16634 message of October 27, 1915, Cobb to State.

53. 812.00/16635 message of October 27, 1915, Cobb to State.

54. Ibid.

55. 812.00/16636 message of October 29, 1915, Cobb to State.

56. 812.00/16625 message of October 29, 1915, Cobb to State.

57. 812.00/16659 message of November 1, 1915, Cobb to State for quote and dissolution of the injunction.

58. 812.00/16729 message of November 6, 1915, Cobb to State.

59. A. J. McQuatters also served as a leader in the Mine and Smelter Operators Association and had praised to Lansing the work of Carothers and Scott during the August talks with Villa. See 812.00/15815 message of August 13, 1915, McQuatters to Lansing, and Hill, *Emissaries*, 348.

60. 812.00/16751 message of November 9, 1915 Cobb to State.

61. 812.00/16754 message of November 4, 1915, Cobb to State. File contains copies of telegrams of Cobb to Treasury, Treasury to Cobb, and Alvarado Mining Company to Treasury.

62. 812.00/16754 message of November 4, 1915, Cobb to State.
63. 812.00/16739 message of November 10, 1915, Cobb to State.
64. 812.00/16760 message of November 10, 1915, Cobb to State.
65. 812.00/16767 message of November 11, 1915, 1 p.m., Cobb to State.
66. Ibid. The internal reference to November 10, 3P, refers to the Treasury instructions contained in /16739 previously cited.
67. 812.00/16770 message of November 11, 1915, 3 p.m., Cobb to State.
68. 812.00/16760 message of November 11, 1915, State to Cobb.
69. 812.00/16775 message of November 12, 1915, Cobb to State.
70. 812.5157/112 letter of December 4, 1915, Cobb to Treasury, later forwarded to State. In arriving at his estimate of profits Villa earned during November, Cobb multiplied each head of cattle by an export fee of $10.00, sheep by $1.00, and each bale of cotton by $10.00 plus miscellaneous taxes to arrive at his figure. However, Cobb did not include profits from the Juárez racetrack of an estimated $100.00 a day or profits from the gambling houses, reportedly the largest in North America, operated by Hipólito Villa.
71. 812.00/16771 message of November 11, 1915, Cobb to State.
72. See 812.113/3770 message of November 15, 1915; 812.00/16829 message of November 20, 1915; /16638 message of November 22, 1915; and /16971 message of December 18, 1915, for details of telegrams between Obregón and Villa commanders. All Cobb to State.
73. See 812.00/16884 message of November 29, 1915, Cobb to State, reporting meeting between Villa faction and eastern mining company representatives; /16885 message of November 29, 1915, Cobb to State, on the movement and intentions of Alvarado Mining Company representative in Chihuahua.
74. 812.00/16853 message of November 24, 1915, Cobb to State, an arriving passenger's report of delays and rerouting fueled speculation "that Luis Herrera with his forces from Parral has occupied Jimenez"; /16902 message of December 2, 1915, Cobb to State, for a report from friends "returning from Chihuahua last night who are reliable and fair" detailing civil and commercial conditions. "American arriving from Torreón" on December 16, 1915 (/16957 Cobb to State), reported Carranza military activities in that area.
75. See 812.00/16848 message of November 23, 1915, Cobb to State, for a report from the inspector at Fort Hancock below El Paso regarding a pending attack by two to three hundred Carranza soldiers on Guadalupe, a nearby Mexican settlement; /16851 message of November 24, 1915, Cobb to State, from the same source reporting a Villista attack on the Carranza soldiers at Cuevo, about twenty miles southeast of Fort Hancock; and /16952 message of December 13, 1915, Cobb to State, with inspector at Fort Hancock reporting discovery of a sabotage attempt on the Southern Pacific and Texas Pacific track.
76. An Associated Press representative identified only as "Arnold, stationed in Nogales [Arizona] temporarily El Paso is of opinion based on talks with

both Randall, the Villa governor, and General Obregón, that Villa is short of commissary and that therefore Villa will probably attempt to take one of the border ports." (812.00/16894 message of December 1, 1915, Cobb to State.)

77. On December 9, 1915 (812.00/16929 Cobb to State), Cobb reported from "authoritative sources" that Villa was not in Madera as reported in press but probably with a force about thirty miles west. Later that day (/16930 message of December 9, 1915, Cobb to State), more details from a "reliable source" indicated Villa would reach Madera on the tenth with four thousand men after looting Dolores. On the tenth Cobb disavowed the numbers with Villa although they were "sufficient to renew menace to State of Chihuahua" (/16935 message of December 10, 1915, Cobb to State). "Unconfirmed reports with appearance of reliable origin" placed Villa with forty men in western Chihuahua. (/17032 message of December 30, 1915, Cobb to State.)

78. 812.00/17083 letter of December 9, 1915, Cobb to Leon J. Canova, head of State Department's Division of Mexican Affairs.

79. 812.00/17083 letter of December 9, 1915, Cobb to Canova.

80. Ibid.

81. 812.00/17083 message of November 24, 1915, Cobb to Treasury. Treasury also forwarded a copy of the letter to State (812.113/3801 message of December 2, 1915), asking, "What else could be done?"

82. 812.00/16866 message of November 26, 1915, Cobb to State. The first warning message to State came two days earlier. (812.00/16851 message of November 24, 1915, Cobb to State.) Simultaneously, Treasury received notice of the local problems noted above.

83. 812.5157/109 message of November 30, 1915, Cobb to State.

84. 812.5157/112 message of December 2, 1915, Cobb to Treasury.

85. Ibid. two of Cobb's letters to the Treasury (December 2 and December 4, 1915), forwarded with a December 9, 1915, cover letter to State under A. J. Peter's signature as acting Treasury Secretary. Peters informed Cobb of the action.

86. Letter of January 30, 1915, Cobb to General Hugh Lennox Scott (Hugh Lennox Scott Papers, Box 17). Scott had favorably brought Cobb to Peters' attention earlier and this letter reflected Cobb's gratitude to Scott.

87. 812.2311/273 message of December 14, 1915, Cobb to State.

88. Ibid.

89. 812.2311/283 message of December 17, 1915, Cobb to State. The message provides copies of local telegrams to Governor Ferguson, Austin's reply, and Cobb's comments to Washington. For original plan see 812.2311/273 message of December 14, 1915, Cobb to State, suggesting using Fabens, with its better facilities, as a crossing site; /282 message of December 17, 1915, Cobb to State, for copies of telegrams between Cobb and Captain Dean at Fort Hancock (not further identified) regarding implementation of the crossing

and cautions of secrecy. Interestingly, local concerns addressed safety and reaction of indigenous Villista sympathizers, not the plan itself, which they did not wish to hamper. The meeting with Cobb may have reflected these genuine concerns and a need for reassurance after Austin's somewhat confused reply.

90. 812.2311/283 message of December 17, 1915, Cobb to State. The quote comes from the El Paso telegram to Governor Ferguson and was meant to significantly reduce the threat of civilian casualties on both sides of the border.

91. See 812.2311/279 message of December 16, 1915, Cobb to State, for awareness of Villa authorities in Juárez of potential troop movements.

92. 812.2311/186 message of December 18, 1915, Cobb to State.

93. See 812.00/15532 message of July 23, 1915, Carothers to State, for sharing of sources, and /15606 message of August 1, 1915, Cobb to State, for quote.

94. See 812.44V71/5 message of September 9, 1915, Carothers to State, for quote, and 812.44V71/4 letter of September 4, 1915, Cobb to Lansing, for copy of and comments on Chocano letter. The Chocano letter is quite interesting. Consul García provided the letter to Cobb originally written to Manuel Bonilla, Villa's representative in Washington, on August 30, 1915. Cobb observed that the two-page letter "is more nearly an accurate estimate of Villa than anything I have ever seen written by a Latin American." "A government built on this man," Chocano said of Villa, "would be an innocent victim sleeping upon grave peril. He listens to no one; he pay [*sic*] no heed to any one, and what is more serious, he believes no one. . . . Can you build a semblance of a government upon such a foundation of psychological lack of equilibrium?"

95. 812.00/16083 message of September 11, 1915, Cobb and Carothers to State. The message indicates that Washington had used the name of the consular agent in Torreón as the source of information on Villa's losses. The local Associated Press correspondent removed the name from the local version of the State Department story.

96. 812.00/16608 message of October 27, 1915, Carothers to State and /16739 message of November 8, 1915, Carothers to State.

97. 812.00/16870 letter of November 22, 1915, Carothers to State.

98. 812.00/24285 letter of December 31, 1915, Cobb to Lansing (one of two letters—same file, date, and correspondents). Consul García provided to a reporter, from seized Villa financial records, a receipt or promissory note from Carothers to Villa for 100,000 pesos. Cobb demanded the receipt for the government and was happy when it could not be produced.

99. Hill, *Emissaries*, 368, cites Lansing's attempted termination of Carothers on December 31, 1915. Hill provides additional background regarding Carothers's declining service on 368–70.

100. 812.00/17002 message of December 23, 1915, Cobb to State.

101. During this period the consul provided an interesting piece of information to Cobb. Seized Villa financial files, the same ones incriminating Carothers,

provided a transaction receipt from "Wyche Greer, formerly manager of the *El Paso Times* to the customs authorities in Juárez, dated about September last, acknowledging receipt of $10,000 paid by direction of Villa authorities and supposed to have been for publicity." (812.00/24285 letter of December 31, 1915, Cobb to Lansing, one of two letters—same file, date, and correspondents.)

102. 812.00/17208 message of December 29, 1915, Cobb to State.
103. See 812.00/17047 message of January 4, 1916, Cobb to State, for quote and outline of visit. 812.00 /17036 message of December 31, 1915, Cobb to State, contains Obregón's crossing.
104. 812.00/24285 letter of December 31, 1915, Cobb to Lansing. The use of VALVI in the text employs a communications filing method lost in the State Department file copies but refers to 812.2311/283 December 17, 1915, previously cited.
105. Ibid.
106. 812.00 24284 letter of December 28, 1915, Cobb to Lansing.
107. 812.00/24285 letter of December 31, 1915, Cobb to Lansing.
108. 812.00/16208 letter of September 17, 1915, Lansing to Cobb.
109. 812.00/24720 letter of September 7, 1915, Lansing to Cobb.
110. 812.00/24284 letter of January 6, 1916, Lansing to Cobb. Cobb often sent clippings from the local paper. Specific clippings associated with this letter cannot be determined.
111. *FRUS, 1915,* 694–95.

CHAPTER 3

1. See 812.00/17054 message of January 15, 1916, and /17098 letter of January 8, 1916, both Cobb to State.
2. See 812.113/3858 message of January 4, 1916, Cobb to State.
3. 812.00/17098 letter of January 8, 1916, Cobb to State. Also see 812.00/17054 message of January 5, 1916, Cobb to State, and 812.515/95 letter of January 7, 1916, Cobb to State, for earlier but less defined statements of Cobb's concerns. The theme of responsibility also occurs in 812.113/3871 message of January 9, 1916, Cobb to State.
4. 812.00/17054 letter of January 15, 1916, State to Cobb, "informed [Cobb] that the Department hopes to fill all consular positions in Mexico in the near future."
5. 812.113/3871 message of January 9, 1916, Cobb to State.
6. 812.00/17098 letter of January 8, 1916, Cobb to State. The referenced "December 29th last" letter is not in the files.
7. W. H. Timmons, *El Paso,* 221.
8. See Louis M. Teitelbaum, *Woodrow Wilson and the Mexican Revolution (1913–1916)* (New York: Exposition Press, 1967), 321, for economic impact

of the Santa Ysabel incident, and 812.00/17114 message of January 18, 1916, and /17117 message of January 19, 1916, both Cobb to State, for Cobb's reporting.

9.   812.00/17193 letter of January 24, 1916, Cobb to Lansing.

10.   Ibid.

11.   812.00/17193 letter of January 29, 1916, Lansing to Cobb. Curiously, considering Lansing's descriptive words regarding Cobb, Barbara Tuchman in *The Zimmermann Telegram* refers to the "indefatigable Agent Cobb in El Paso," 182, and John Mason Hart in *Revolutionary Mexico*, calls Cobb "the zealous anti-Villista head of U.S. Customs," 270. Lansing's use of the term "environment of criticism" may well have referred to the Treasury Department. A copy of the letter was provided to Treasury Secretary William MacAdoo the same day via cover letter "commending him [Cobb] for good work which he has been doing for this Department, in connection with the situation in Mexico." See same decimal file, letter of January 29, 1916, Lansing to MacAdoo.

12.   Message of January 21, 1916, Cobb to State, Records of the Department of State Relating to Internal Affairs of Germany, 1910–1929, Department of State Decimal Files, Series 862.20212/1, National Archives Microfilm Publication M336, rolls 55–59; General Records of the Department of State, Record Group 59. Hereafter cited as 862.20212/appropriate number.

13.   862.20212/1 message of January 21, 1916, Cobb to State.

14.   Ibid.

15.   862.20212/1 letter of January 24, 1916, State to Justice.

16.   862.20212/1 White House memorandum of January 24, 1916, Wilson to Lansing.

17.   862.20212/1 letter of January 27, 1916, Lansing to Wilson. Despite an initially slow reaction, indicated in differences between the letter to Justice of January 24, and the January 27 response to the president, State did forward copies to the Department of War on January 27, and to the American Consul in Vera Cruz on February 1 (both 862.20212/1), and, as an indicator of its significance, opened a new decimal file within Records of the Department of State Relating to Internal Affairs of Germany, 1910–29, Series 862.

18.   862.20212/1 message of January 28, 1916, State to Cobb.

19.   862.20212/3 message of February 6, 1916, Cobb to State.

20.   862.20212/3 message of February 8, 1916, State to Cobb.

21.   862.20212/11 message of April 20, 1916, Cobb to State.

22.   862.20212/11 message of April 24, 1916, Lansing to Cobb.

23.   Robert Lansing, *War Memoirs of Robert Lansing, Secretary of State* (New York: Bobbs-Merrill Co., 1935), 318–19.

24.   For theories on the Villa raid see Harris and Sadler, *The Border and the Revolution*, 101–9; Friedrich Katz, "Pancho Villa and the Attack of Columbus, New Mexico," *American Historical Review* (hereafter *AHR*) 83 (February

1978): 116, and James A. Sandos, "German Involvement in Northern Mexico, 1915–1916: A New Look at the Columbus Raid," *HAHR* 50 (February 1970): 70–78.

25. 812.00/16929 message of December 9, 1915, Cobb to State. Modern maps list the town as Mader*a*. Cobb uses the spelling Mader*o* in his telegrams. Both refer to the same town.

26. 812.00/16930 message of December 9, 1915, Cobb to State.

27. See 812.00/16935 message of December 10, 1915, and /16941 message of December 12, 1915, both Cobb to State. In the first, Cobb found Villa's strength impossible to determine but "sufficient to renew menace to State of Chihuahua and American interest there." In the second, "Best evidence" indicated a strength of twenty-five hundred but of unknown loyalty and intentions. Carothers reported that Villa would not come to the border but would go to Torreón. (812.00/16938 message of December 12, 1915, Carothers to State.) Consul Thomas Edwards in Juárez reported Villa with four thousand men. (812.00/16942 message of December 12, 1915, Edwards to State.) The weekly report from Fort Bliss, mirroring Cobb, placed Villa in Madera on the tenth with twenty-five hundred troops. (812.00/16979 for the week of December 11, 1915.)

28. See 812.2311/286 message of December 18, 1915; 812.00/16978 message of December 20, 1915; /16982 message of December 21, 1915; and /16991 message of December 22, 1915, all Cobb to State, for information on the Villa family in El Paso.

29. 812.00/16978 message of December 20, 1915, for first quote, and 812.2311/286 message of December 18, 1915, for second quote. Both Cobb to State.

30. 812.2311/286 message of December 18, 1915, Cobb to State. Use of the phrase "personally intended" and preceding material in the message addressing the Villa family (see above) indicate the family as the source.

31. 812.00/16971 message of December 18, 1915, Cobb to State.

32. 812.00/16978 message of December 20, 1915, Cobb to State. See 812.00/16973 message of December 19, 1915, and /16976 message of December 20, 1915, both Cobb to State, for statements reinforcing the idea of Villa's peacefully crossing the border.

33. 812.00/16982 message of December 21, 1915, Cobb to State. The beginning of the message essentially listed the Villa family and covered their departure to Havana via New Orleans. The presence and level of this detail indicates the family as the source of information regarding Villa.

34. 812.00/16991 message of December 22, 1915, Cobb to State.

35. 812.00/7032 message of December 30, 1915, Cobb to State. The army would not report Villa in Buenaventura until their weekly report for February 26, 1916. (812.00/17358.) See 812.00/17037 message of December 31, 1915, for follow-up background and comments from Cobb on the size of Villa's force.

36. See 812.00/17066 message of January 8, 1916, Cobb to State, for crossing report.
37. 812.00/17091 message of January 13, 1916, Cobb to State.
38. See 812.00/17087 message of January 13, 1916, 4 p.m., Cobb to State, for ammunition report. An earlier message that same day was based on the railroad agent in Madera. (/17092 message of January 13, 1916, 11 a.m., Cobb to State.) Timing and geography lend support to similar sources for the two messages. State instructed Cobb to convey the information to Mexican authorities. (/17087 file.) Cobb may have complied as he subsequently reported capture of the ammunition. (/17184 message of January 30, 1916, Cobb to State.)
39. 812.00/17146 letter of January 19, 1916, Cobb to State. The letter also reported Villa's strength as between 100 and 1,500 men.
40. 812.00/17164 message of January 27, 1916, Cobb to State. Villa's strength was reported "as numbering all the way from one hundred men up."
41. 812.00/17125 message of January 20, 1916, Cobb to State. The Fort Bliss weekly report for January 22, 1916, would report Villa's capture as false. (812.00/17194.)
42. 812.00/17345 letter of February 8, 1916, Cobb to State. This document provides excerpts from three internal American Mining and Smelting Company letters dated January 31 (quoted above), February 1, and February 2, provided to Cobb by the general manager.
43. 812.00/17214 message of February 3, 1916, and /17215 message of February 4, 1916, both Cobb to State.
44. See 812.00/17190 and /17197 messages of February 1, 1916, Cobb to State, for robbery and Ojinaga movement, and /17208 message of February 3, 1916, for Gallego movement. The executed former compatriot was Gen. Tomás Orñelas. (File /17190.)
45. 812.00/17208 message of February 3, 1916, Cobb to State. However, Cobb reported the wires cut the next day. (/17211 message of February 4, 1916, Cobb to State.)
46. Katz, "Pancho Villa and the Attack on Columbus," *AHR*, 116.
47. 812.00/17302 message of February 21, 1916, Cobb to State.
48. 812.00/17340 message of March 3, 1916, Cobb to State.
49. 812.00/17355 message of March 6, 1916, Cobb to State.
50. 812.00/17361 message of March 7, 1916, Cobb to State.
51. 812.00/17369 message of March 8, 1916, 3 p.m., Cobb to State. First message is /17368 of March 8, 1916, 2 p.m., Cobb to State, which, based on private sources in Juárez, pointed out that Villa had not been attacked or pursued due to insufficient local forces.
52. 812.00/17377 message of March 9, 1916, State to Consul John R. Silliman.
53. See 812.00/17459 letter of March 8, 1916, Cobb to State, addressing activities of Manuel Calero in an article titled "PLAN under which the FEDERAL

ARMY OF THE REPUBLIC OF MEXICO proposes to restore public order and peace throughout the Republic, as well as the Constitutional Regime."

54. 812.00/17377 message of March 9, 1916, Cobb to State. See /17385 message of March 9, 1916, Cobb to State, for indication that Riggs telephoned his report.

55. Notes on 812.00/17377 message of March 9, 1916, Cobb to State, for confirmation, and Gilderhus, *Diplomacy and Revolution*, 35, for meeting.

56. 812.00/17382 message of March 9, 1916, State to Silliman. Also see Hill, *Emissaries*, 371.

57. 812.00/17378 message of March 9, 1916, 10 a.m., Cobb to State. Cobb received the information regarding coordination and accuracy in a phone call from Riggs.

58. 812.00/17385 message of March 9, 1916, 10 a.m., Cobb to State. Second report of the day.

59. Ibid. For Cobb's preraid attitude on intervention see 812.00/17098 letter of January 8, 1916, /17193 letter of January 24, 1916, and /17178 letter of January 25, 1916, all Cobb to State.

60. 812.00/17386 message of March 9, 1916, 4 p.m., Cobb to State. Third report of the day.

61. 812.00/17387 message of March 9, 1916, 5 p.m., Cobb to State. Fourth and final report of the day.

62. 812.00/17404 message of March 10, 1916, 5 p.m., Cobb to State.

63. See 812.00/17403 of March 10, and /17421 of March 11 for additional border violations; 812.721/31 of March 10, 812.00/17423 of March 11, and /17436 of March 12 for telegraph problems; /17424 of March 11 for report of southerly troop movements; and /17427 of March 11 for the contents of the diary—all 1916 messages, Cobb to State. The diary covers the writer's movements during the Santa Ysabel incident and parallels Cobb's reports of Villa's movements prior to Columbus. Background to the diary, long lost in the National Archives, can be found in Harris and Sadler, *The Border and the Revolution*, 101–9.

64. 812.00/17395 message of March 10, 1916, 8 p.m., Cobb to State. See /17404 message of March 10, 1916, 5 p.m., for Mexican troop movements.

65. 812.00/17408 message of March 10, 1916, 8 p.m., Cobb to State.

66. 812.00/17542 message of March 13, 1916, Cobb to State.

67. 812.00/17396 report of March 10, 1916, Gen. Frederick Funston to Adjutant General, Washington.

68. Katz, "Pancho Villa and the Attack on Columbus," *AHR,* 102.

69. Ibid.

70. 812.00/17486 message of March 14, 1916, Cobb to State.

71. 812.00/17468 message of March 14, 1916, Cobb to State.

72. 812.00/17498 message of March 16, 1916, Cobb to State.

73. 812.00/17676 message of March 30, 1916, State to U.S. Consul, Chihuahua, Mexico.

74. 812.00/17691 message of March 30, 1916, Cobb to State.

75. Ibid. Cobb subsequently confirmed Villa's location, strength, and direction of late March and, along with similar information on Carrancista forces, passed the same to General Bell, the local commander. (/17716 message of April 1, 1916, Cobb to State.)

76. 812.00/17705 message of March 31, 1916, Cobb to State.

77. Clendenen, *Blood on the Border*, 245.

78. 812.00/17727 message of April 3, 1916, 3 p.m., Cobb to State.

79. 812.00/17740 message of April 3, 1916, 8 a.m., Cobb for Consul Letcher at Chihuahua to State.

80. 812.00/17728 message of April 3, 1916, 6 p.m., Cobb to State.

81. 812.00/17812 message of April 11, 1916, Cobb to State, reported "that Villa entered the house of Andrés Rahaza to take a girl and that in defending girl Rahaza shot Villa in knee after which Rahaza was killed. However, this letter is a week old and there is no conclusive confirmation that Villa was ever shot."

82. 812.00/18650 message of July 5, 1916, Cobb to State. This message confirmed /18642 of July 4, 1916. Each message appears to originate with separate travelers coming to El Paso from Mexico. Contrary to this report, Villa was indeed hit in a leg bone. See 812.00/20760 letter of March 14, 1917, Cobb to State, for Cobb's report from an attending physician of bone damage to Villa's leg.

83. See 812.00/17875 message of April 16, 1916, Cobb to State, for the Mexican reports and sources of Villa's death, and /17893 message of April 17, 1916, Cobb to State, for doctor and dentist consultations. The later message contains some technical details of Villa's dental work. One of Cobb's sources, Patrick O'Hea, may have provided an early lead on Villa's teeth based on a previous experience. See Patrick O'Hea, *Reminiscences of the Mexican Revolution* (Mexico City: Centro Anglo–Mexicano del Libro, 1966), 169–70.

84. For background on these talks see Gilderhus, *Diplomacy and Revolution*, 40–42, and John S. D. Eisenhower, *Intervention: The United States and the Mexican Revolution, 1913–1917* (New York: W. W. Norton and Co., 1993), 281–86.

85. Cobb mentions leaving the next day in a message of April 26, 1916. (812.00/17977.) His next communication occurs on May 27, 1916. (812.00/18532.)

86. 812.00/17578 message of March 22, 1916, Cobb to State.

87. 812.00/18438 message of June 15, 1916, Cobb to State.

88. Cobb's commentary on the two families is too extensive to list individually but see 812.00/19026 letter of August 23, 1916, Cobb to State, for the Treviños, and /19027 same date and parties for the Herreras.

89. 812.00/18865 message of August 5, 1916, Cobb to State.
90. 812.515/99 letter of March 25, 1916, Cobb to State.
91. 812.515/83 letter of October 26, 1916, Cobb to State.
92. 812.00/20457 message of January 30, 1917, Cobb to State.
93. See as examples 812.51/243 message of April 6, 1916, Cobb to State, for gold; 812.63/204 letter of September 18, 1916, Cobb to Treasury, for silver; and 812.00/19274 message of September 24, 1916, Cobb to State, for the wife of General Jacinto Treviño declaring her jewelry on entering the United States.
94. See 812.00/18726 message of July 14, 1916, for Mexican government blaming merchants for food shortage, 812.50/19 message of July 20, 1916, for merchant protest, and 812.515/147 message of July 25, 1916, for governmental attempts at price control. All Cobb to State.
95. 812.00/19507 letter of September 6, 1916, Cobb to State.
96. Knight, *The Mexican Revolution*, 1:411.
97. 812.00/19103 message of September 9, 1916, State to Cobb.
98. 812.00/19217 letter of September 14, 1916, Cobb to State.
99. Knight, *The Mexican Revolution*, 1:413.
100. 812.00/19661 message of October 20, 1916, State to Cobb, Carothers, and Edwards. See /19661 message of October 28, 1916, Lansing to Franklin K. Lane, Secretary of the Interior and U.S. head of the Joint Commission, for the Joint Commission as the source of the request. For details of the Joint Commission see Gilderhus, *Diplomacy and Revolution*, 47–49.
101. 812.00/19683 message of October 29, 1916, 8 p.m., Edwards to State.
102. 812.00/19719 message of November 2, 1916, Carothers to State.
103. 812.00/19860 message of October 29, 1916, Cobb to State.
104. 812.00/18231 letter of February 20, 1916, Cobb to State. Later in the letter he wrote, "I told him [the merchant] that personally I would like to meet Calero and talk with him, but was not at liberty to do so—that if I met him it would be misunderstood by him or others."

CHAPTER 4

1. Haley, *Revolution and Intervention*, 255.
2. For example see 812.00/19739 message of November 4, 1916, for use of a German doctor; /19839 message of November 11, 1916, for use of a French traveler; and especially /19677 letter of October 17, 1916, from a British official in Mexico City reporting on Carranza's family fleeing Mexico.
3. See 812.00/19778 message of November 9, 1916, Lansing to Cobb, for the assignment; /19871 letter of November 10, 1916, Cobb to State, for processing to Chihuahua; and /19903 letter of November 13, 1916, Cobb to State, for completion via a signed receipt.

4. See 812.113/5197 letter of November 15, 1916, Cobb to State.

5. 812.113/5485 letter of December 15, 1916, Cobb to State, for quote. Baron was normally identified by the sobriquet "our man in Chihuahua" prior to this point.

6. 812.113/5197 letter of November 15, 1916, Cobb to State.

7. 862.20212/572 letter of August 2, 1917, Cobb to State.

8. For Cobb's messages forwarded to Mexico City see 862.20212/489 message of July 17, regarding German agents in Mexico; 812.113/8807 message of August 8, regarding General Murguía's attendance at a picnic highlighting German officials; /8920 message of August 17, on transfer of Murguía; 862.20212/546 message of August 22, indicating Carranza's change of officials in Chihuahua; /611 message of September 13, pertaining to propaganda material from the Indian National Party entering the United States from Mexico; /814d message of November 12, indicating possible removal of German nationals from the Mexican side of the border—all 1917, State to U.S. embassy, Mexico City.

9. 862.20212/537 message of August 16, 1916, Cobb to State. The incident involved Governor Arnulfo Gonzales's trip to Los Angeles to confer with German bankers.

10. 862.20212/51 message of December 28, 1916, Cobb to State.

11. See Katz, *Secret War in Mexico*, 391–95.

12. See 862.20212/51 which contains a letter of January 3, 1917, State to War, requesting suspension of the army investigation; an internal memo of January 3, 1917, Chief of Staff to the Adjutant General, indicating the Secretary of War's compliance with State's request; and a message of January 10, 1917, State to Cobb, directing a rush report.

13. 862.20212/52 message of January 11, 1917, Cobb to State.

14. 862.20212/52 message of January 12, 1917, State to Cobb, for quote; and /51 memorandum of January 12, 1917, State to War, for permission to countermand instructions to suspend the army investigation.

15. See Katz, *Secret War in Mexico*, 433; and O'Toole, *Honorable Treachery*, 269. O'Toole cites Katz as the source of his information.

16. For indications of Cobb's coordination with other agencies see 862.20212/68 letter of February 7, 1917, Cobb to State; 862.20212/154 message of March 30, 1917, Cobb to State; and 862.20212/760 letter of October 2, 1917, Cobb to State, noting cooperation with Justice and army and also subsequent incidents in this chapter. In the last example, Cobb shared with army and Justice information from one of his very special agents, Mr. N., whose identity was carefully safeguarded.

17. 862.20212/55 message of January 13, 1917, Cobb to State.

18. See 812.00/20205 letter of December 20, 1916, Cobb to State, which voiced alarm over Mexican impressions of General Bell's assumed authority as "a confusion that may lead to misunderstanding in some more serious thing."

19. For information on the Zimmermann telegram see Tuchman, *The Zimmermann Telegram*, and David Kahn, *The Codebreakers* (New York: Macmillan Co., 1967), 282–97.

20. Tuchman, *The Zimmermann Telegram*, 146.

21. 862.20212/77 message of March 1, 1917, 2 p.m., Cobb to State.

22. Tuchman, *The Zimmermann Telegram,* 182.

23. 812.00/20256 1/2 letter of January 4, 1917, Cobb to State. Despite its reference to German relations with Mexico, this letter is in the Mexican rather than German file. Additional information from the interviews is reported in 812.00/20233 letter of January 4, 1916, Cobb to State.

24. 812.00/20256 1/2 letter of January 4, 1917, Cobb to State. Notably, in presenting Kock's story, Cobb accepts Kock's explanation of Villa's payment to his troops in captured silver rather than reports from other sources that the silver came from German sources.

25. 812.00/20546 message of February 20, 1917, Cobb to State, reported reopening of communication with Parral and, "Difficult ascertain whereabouts and immediate purposes of Villa." /20552 message of February 21, 1917, Cobb to State, reported, "Whereabouts Villa puzzling. Científico Mexicans believe he is in State Of Durango." /20563 message of February 23, 1917, Cobb to State, reported, "Mexicans circulating confusing reports placing Villa sick in Durango, west of Carrizal assembling ammunition hidden in Pershing territory [Pershing left Mexico February 5] and even that he has been to San Francisco with agents of Cantú [Mexican governor in Baja]. Most probably north of Chihuahua contemplating attack on trains or [*sic*–to?] Juárez or Ojinaga."

26. 812.00/21425 letter of September 25, 1917, Cobb to State. Cobb's concern with protecting the identity of his sources reflects frequent breaches of security at the State Department. Lansing notes the problem and creation of a photo pass system to enter the building housing the department and restrictions on the press to individual personnel. (Lansing, *War Memoirs*, 320–21.)

27. 812.63/254 letter of October 19, 1916, Cobb to State.

28. 812.00/20256 1/2 letter of January 4, 1917, Cobb to State. Cobb returned to the theme of the Germans playing Mexican factions in his report of March 1, 1917 (862.20212/77) indicating German support for Villa, and a report of March 3 (862.20212/82).

29. 812.113/4992 message of October 13, 1916, Cobb to State, for quote and same file for affirmative response from State the next day.

30. 812.00/19739 message of November 4, 1916, Cobb to State. Also see /20211 letter of December 24, 1916, Cobb to State which describes Villa as having more ammunition than Carranza forces but debunks Villa's claim of 14 million rounds of ammunition buried in Chihuahua.

31. See 812.113/5660 report of January 16, 1917, Justice to State, in response to "complaints made by Mexican officials and others as to lack of enforcement of the embargo on munitions of war into Mexico." The report covers in

some detail the efforts of War, Justice, and Customs agents on the border to prevent ammunition smuggling. Also see 812.113/6160 letter of January 17, 1917, Cobb to State, an eight-page report on the operation of one recently exposed smuggling ring, and /5946 letter of February 13, 1917, Cobb to Treasury, requesting guidance regarding his enforcement powers and stating, "we are too aware that ammunition is getting by, in spite of all that we can do to prevent the same, under power possessed by us."

32. 812.113/5164 message of February 3, 1917, Cobb to State.
33. See 812.113/5807 memo of February 8, 1917, War to State, concurring with Cobb's proposal, and a letter of February 10, 1917, State to Cobb, requesting specific railroads to contact.
34. See 812.113/6068 letter of February 17, 1917, Cobb to State, for Cobb's response; /5907 message of March 10, 1917, State to Cobb, for action in contacting five railroad presidents.
35. See 812.113/6074, /6075, and /6093 of March 12 and 13, 1917, for affirmative responses of cooperation from railroads.
36. See 812.113/5890 message of February 21, /5907 message of February 23, /5960 letter of February 23, /5924 message of February 25, and /5948 message of February 27 (all 1917 and Cobb to State), for general examples of implementation; and /5972 message of March 1, 1917, Cobb to State, for cooperation of railroad to bluff local merchant, Henry Mohr, into returning ammunition to shipper.
37. 812.113/6119 message of March 15, 1917, Cobb to State.
38. 812.113/6195 letter of March 17, 1917, Cobb to State.
39. 812.113/6243 letter of March 19, 1917, Treasury to Cobb, enclosed in a Cobb to State letter of March 19, 1917.
40. 812.113/6243 letter of March 23, 1917, Cobb to State.
41. 812.113/6356 message of April 2, 1917, Pershing to Adjutant General.
42. 812.113/6634; Pershing's order is contained in a letter of April 20, 1917, Cobb to General Bell.
43. 812.113/6634 letter of April 20, 1917, Cobb to Bell.
44. See 812.113/5713 letter of January 18, 1917, Cobb to State. The plant was supposedly at full capacity and had stocks of crude and manufactured articles including soda nitrate, potash, nitric acid, black powder, smokeless powder, and dynamite.
45. 812.113/5815 letter of February 5, 1917, Cobb to State.
46. 812.113/6190 letter of March 13, 1917, Cobb to State.
47. Ibid. Gutiérrez indicated that bulk ammunition could not be obtained from Japan due to the pressure of the U.S. State Department on the government of Japan to prevent its shipment.
48. See 812.113/6012 letter of February 27, 1917, Cobb to State, for the first identification of Gottwald. This letter references an earlier, unlocated January 31 report also identifying him. Gottwald dominates 812.113/6108 letter

of March 2,1917, Cobb to State. 862.20212/172 letter of March 27, 1917, Cobb to State, involves Gottwald with another El Paso firm, Krakauer, Zork, and Moye, in selling ammunition.

49. 862.20212/164 letter of March 29, 1917, Cobb to State, for quote. The information came from "An American employee of the Carranza government, who called at the office yesterday, . . . based upon impressions gathered by him from Mexicans associated with the government." Gottwald's brewery background is in 812.113/6108 letter of March 2, 1917, Cobb to State.

50. 862.20212/151 message of March 29, 1917, Cobb to State.

51. See 862.20212/186 message of April 5, 1917, Cobb to State, for arrest report, and /176 message of April 4, for vague warning of event. Justice may, of course, have previously installed a tap on Gottwald's phone.

52. See 862.20212/192 message of April 7, 1917, Cobb to State.

53. Cobb's primary concern was keeping Gottwald in jail and preventing his release as a potential sign of encouragement to others. Accordingly, Cobb emphasized suspension of habeas corpus, rearrest on additional charges, and declaring Gottwald an enemy alien–difficult since he claimed Mexican citizenship of more than twenty years. See 862.20212/240 message of April 16, 1917; /247 message of April 18, 1917; /254 message of April 19, 1917; and /290 letter of April 26, 1917, with attached court documents and Cobb's explanatory comments. All Cobb to State.

54. Cobb's reports are far too numerous to list separately, but see 862.20212/127 message of March 23, 862.20212/154 message of March 30, 812.00/20769 message of April 9, 812.515/187 letter of April 17, and 812.5151/98 letter of May 12, as examples. All 1917 and Cobb to State. Also note distribution of information in various files.

55. 812.515/197 letter of July 24, 1917, MacAdoo to Lansing. Profits would have amounted to over two hundred thousand dollars for both the Mexican government and Iselin over a two-year period.

56. At least, while aware of rumors of the connection between the Mint and Mexican gold, Cobb makes no mention of official knowledge. See 812.5151/98 letter of May 12, 1917, Cobb to State.

57. 812.00/20874 letter of April 24, 1917, Cobb to State.

58. See 812.00/20899 letter of April 27, 1917, Cobb to State, for several graphic pictures of clusters of men hung reportedly at Murguía's orders; and 862.20212/696 letter of August 1, 1917, Cobb to State, indicating Murguía's public slapping of his personal adjutant and the latter's immediate suicide.

59. Two other agents, named Plumb (see 812.00/21025 letter of June 7, 1917, Cobb to State) and Murray (see 862.20212/429 of July 6, 1917, Cobb to State) surface but gain no distinct identity.

60. See 862.20212/311 letter of May 2, 1917, Cobb to State, and /565 letter of August 2, 1917, Cobb to State, for broad lists of Germans and their activities

from Nesgaard. Nesgaard's initial information listed four German suspects and provided information on a "Japanese captain" operating near Murguía.

61. 862.20212/311 letter of May 2, 1917, Cobb to State.

62. 862.20212/570 letter of August 2, 1917, Cobb to State.

63. See Katz, *Secret War*, 437.

64. See 862.20212/558 letter of August 16, 1917, Cobb to State, where a Justice agent, Victor Weiskopf, used a Mexican telegrapher to discover Rueter's application for use of the system as a press correspondent. See /790 September 22, 1917, Cobb to State, in which Cobb reports, "a Mexican in the telegraph office in Juárez, who was eager to furnish us with all German messages, for a consideration, has been unable to find any. It is probable that the messages are sent from Chihuahua to Mexico City by wireless, so that they will not pass through the hands of various operators." Based on this same report Katz incorrectly asserts, "In order to be sure that all of the consul's [Rueter's] secrets were known, Cobb also bribed an employee of the Mexican telegraph office in Ciudad Juárez, who gave him copies of all telegrams sent and received by the consul." (Katz, *Secret War*, 438.) Finally, in June Cobb indicated a suspicion that the Mexican consul in El Paso had used the Mexican wires to transmit information but did not indicate any ability to ascertain or obtain same, indicating little ability to infiltrate the Mexican system at that time. (See 862.20212/437 of June 29, 1917.)

65. 862.20212/759 letter of October 2, 1917, Cobb to State.

66. 862.20212/685 letter of October 5, 1917, Cobb to State.

67. Cobb again asked State to obtain permission granting him access to censored mail on October 13 (862.20212/731) but received no reply.

68. For examples of Nesgaard's list of suspect Germans see 862.20212/311 letter of May 2, 1917, Cobb to State; /565 letter of August 2, 1917, Cobb to State; 812.74/106 letter of August 31, 1917, Cobb to State.

69. 862.20212/676 letter of September 22, 1917, Cobb to State.

70. Ibid.

71. 862.20212/742 letter of October 2, 1917, Cobb to State.

72. 862.20212/908 letter of January 5, 1918, Cobb to State.

73. See 862.20212/761 letter of October 2, 1917, Cobb to State.

74. 812.74/57 letter of February 7, 1917, Cobb to State.

75. Cobb reported the interference with army systems in 812.74/57 letter of February 7, but may have started his awareness of the problem as early as July 1916. The Fort Bliss Provost Marshal report of July 16, 1916 (Pershing Papers, Box 372), states, "The wire-less station now being constructed in Juárez is being built for the Villa Government for purposes for their own communication. The present plant is a small one pole plant with a small radius. The new plant is to be more powerful and is expected as far south as Aguascalientes." Information from Cobb regarding a possible escape plan for Huerta is in the same report.

76. 862.20212/654 letter of August 17, 1917, Cobb to State.
77. 862.20212/106 letter of August 31, 1917, Cobb to State.
78. 812.74/116 letter of October 15, 1917, Cobb to State. Cobb suspected the Nordwalds of being possible German agents. (862.20212/565 letter of August 2, 1917, Cobb to State.) For the height of the tower, see 862.20212/761 letter of October 2, 1917, Cobb to State.
79. 812.74/121 letter of December 5, 1917, Cobb to State. Same file for range of the old facility; /122 letter of October 13, 1917, Cobb to State, for Cobb's intent to prevent wireless supplies from crossing the border for the new tower; and /125 letter of January 5, 1918, Cobb to State, for operational date.
80. 862.20212/570 letter of August 2, 1917, Cobb to State. See 862.20212/515 message of August 6, 1917, Cobb to State, for report on social events and list of dignitaries.
81. 862.20212/546 letter of August 13, 1917, Cobb to State.
82. 812.00/21425 letter of September 25, 1917, Cobb to State.
83. 812.119/34 letter of June 9, 1917, Cobb to Lansing.
84. 862.20212/785 letter of October 29, 1917, Cobb to State.
85. 862.20212/765 letter of November 1, 1917, Cobb to State.
86. Ibid.
87. Ibid.
88. See 862.20212/608 letter of September 1, 1917, Cobb to State. State expressed interest in this idea. (Same file, letter of September 26, 1917, Lansing to Cobb.)
89. See letter of September 18, 1918, Records of the Department of State, Purport Lists for the Department of State Decimal File, 1910–1944, Series 119.251, File: Administration of the U.S. Government, Organization, Function, etc., Zachery (*sic*) L. Cobb, Special Agent, Department of State, Number 111.70C63/1. National Archives Microfilm Publication M973, roll 13; General Records of the Department of State, Record Group 59. Hereafter cited as decimal number/file number.
90. See 111.70C63/3 message of October 18, 1918, Cobb at Piedras Negras to State requesting his salary, and /8 message of October 26, 1918, State to Cobb, announcing check mailed. The paucity of entries prohibits full evaluation of Cobb's salary or duties. He may have only received expenses and a stipend when on assignment.
91. Most of Cobb's reports provided by the State Department to Van Deman were returned. Of the reports still in MID files, several deserve mention. Records of the Military Intelligence Division, Record Group 165, contains a series of November 1917 reports for Galentine, Sr., from Chihuahua (hereafter identified as MID file number). These were apparently hand delivered by Cobb to State and do not appear in State files. The Chihuahua wireless is the dominant subject. Copies of Cobb's photographs of and the basic report on the wireless facility from 812.74/116 are in MID 6264–106, letter of October 15, 1917.

92. MID 9700-416 letter of January 17, 1918, Lansing to Attorney General Thomas W. Gregory. Lansing's letter refers several times to a Cobb letter of December 21, 1917, defining the problem and solution to Germans carrying military information across the border. Lansing endorsed the proposal and legislation. State followed up the initial Cobb suggestion with a second letter on January 21, 1918 (same MID file, Polk to AG), indicating support from Arizona Representative Carl Hayden.
93. MID 10439–1 letter of December 11, 1917, Cobb to Van Deman.
94. See 812.00/21504 letter of November 7, 1917, Harry W. Cannon for Cobb to State, for an example of subordinates reporting for Cobb; /783 letter of November 12, 1917, Cobb to State, for Cobb's use of War Trade Board (WTB) stationery to report information from Baron while in Washington; 812.00/22089 letter of June 26, 1917, for an example of customs in El Paso continuing to report to State. It is interesting to note that Paul Fuller, whom Cobb met in El Paso while Fuller acted as an agent for the president, served as director of the WTB. (812.00/21464 for Fuller on WTB letterhead.)

CHAPTER 5

1. *El Paso Herald*, March 1, 1918. The new district, according to Cobb, included El Paso, Hudspeth, Culberson, Reeves, Loving, Winkler, Andrews, Martin, Howard, Mitchell, Coke, Tom Green, Menard, Mason, Gillespie, Kerr, Bandera, Real, Edwards, Val Verde, Terrell, Brewster, and Presidio counties in West Texas. (Love Papers, A50.104, Box 8, Correspondence 1918–1919, Folder 6, letter of May 11, 1918, Cobb to Thomas B. Love, assistant secretary of the treasury.)
2. *El Paso Morning Times*, April 1, 1918.
3. 111.70C63/11 (Zachery L. Cobb, Special Agent, Department of State) message of April 15, 1918, Cobb to State. Cobb reported the commitment to Washington as it delayed his departure to Washington as a State Department special representative. State approved the delay the following day. (Same file.)
4. *El Paso Herald*, April 5, 1918.
5. Campaign flyer, Love Papers, File A50.104, Correspondence 1918–1919, C. Correspondence Folder.
6. Ibid.
7. *El Paso Herald*, April 5, 1918.
8. *El Paso Morning Times*, July 21, 24, 25, and 27. The headlines started on July 3 and ran until July 27.
9. *El Paso Herald*, July 9, 1918.
10. *El Paso Morning Times*, July 25, 1918. Cobb had not paid any taxes on the acreage since 1914 and only $39.20 on a lot valued at $2,200 in the Franklin

Heights area.

11. The small headline in *El Paso Morning Times*, July 20, 1918, read "Means Says he is responsible for downfall Huerta." Gaston B. Means worked for a local detective agency and claimed responsibility for the arrest. His role, if any, appears minor.

12. *El Paso Herald*, April 5, 1918.

13. Letter of May 13, 1918, Love to Cobb in Love Papers, File A50.104, Correspondence 1918–1919, C. Correspondence Folder. Cobb responded in a letter of May 11 (same file), "If you mark your reply confidential, it will be received by my wife and guarded as such here."

14. Campaign flyer in Love Papers, File A50.104, Correspondence 1918–1919, C. Correspondence Folder.

15. Confidential letter of May 15, 1918, Cobb to Love in Love Papers, A50.104 Box 8, Correspondence 1918–1919, C. Correspondence Folder.

16. Ibid.

17. Letter of July 15, 1918, Love to Tumulty in Love Papers, A50.104, Box 8, Correspondence 1918-1919, C. Correspondence Folder,

18. See Lewis Gould, *Progressives and Prohibitionists: Texas Democrats in the Wilson Era* (Austin: Texas State Historical Assoc., 1992), 243: "The hands off policy carried over into the race for the Sixteenth District around El Paso. Former collector of customs and sometimes Mexican diplomat Zach Lamar Cobb, opposed C. B. Hudspeth, a Bailey ally and critic of Wilson. 'If possible,' Cobb informed Love in late June, 'I want a letter from the President.' " [Based on a July 12, 1918, letter Cobb to Love.]

19. Letter of July 13, 1918, Cobb to Love in Love Papers, A50.104, Box 8, Correspondence 1918–1919, C. Correspondence Folder.

20. *El Paso Morning Times,* July 26, 1918.

21. *El Paso Herald*, July, 29, 1918.

22. Letter of July 31, 1918, Cobb to Love in Love Papers, A50.104, Box 8, Correspondence 1918–1919, C. Correspondence Folder.

23. The *El Paso Herald* of September 13, 1918, reported, "Mr. Cobb has been recommended by officials of the government and Texas senators for an important post at New York."

24. See 812.00/22475 letter of January 22, 1919; /22502 letter of February 7, 1919; /22173 letter of February 19, 1919; and 812.2311/354 letter of May 28, 1919, all Cobb to State, on War Trade Board letterhead for examples of Cobb's continued intelligence view of the border and direct reporting to State.

25. Records of the Bureau of Exports, Records of the Trade Division, Country File Mexico, Box 431, Record Group 182, message of March 28, 1918, Cobb to State (hereafter cited as WTB —). State forwarded a copy of the message to the War Trade Board. An original is not found in State Department files. Cobb's February 21, 1919, letter relaxing newsprint export regulations can be found in the same file.

26. For Dulles's action on newsprint see WTB, Box 431, memorandum of August 29, 1918. For Van Deman's request see WTB, Box 38, letter number 138 of April 16, 1918, Van Deman, Chief, Military Intelligence Branch, General Staff to Captain Dulles, WTB. The letter stated, "By reason of this gap, it is necessary for the Mexican forces at the important border point of Ojinaga to use the telegraph service at Presidio, Texas. The censorship of all dispatches through the Presidio office is a valuable source of information to us."

27. See 111.70C63/12. (Zachery L. Cobb, Special Agent, Department of State.) Apparently as a part of a move toward resignation, Cobb requested to keep his old files (August 20, 1919); State instructed files be turned over to consul in Juárez (September 26, 1919), and consul in Juárez reported delivery of the files (September 24, 1919). Date discrepancies are in the original records and could not be resolved. All records stored in the consulate were destroyed in a fire on December 24, 1922. Presumably Cobb's records were also. See letter of April 21, 1936, Juárez Consulate to State, responding to Department's Diplomatic Serial No. 2633 of April 13, 1936, File Number 124.00/212 on "submission of information concerning the space used in the Ciudad Juárez Consulate for currently useful archives and for those which might be ordered shipped to the National Archives in Washington."

28. See MID 2338-0184 letter of May 21, 1920, MID to Cobb. No return questionnaire or subsequent information from Cobb appears in the file. The letter referred to Cobb as an "authority of Mexico," yet initial inquiry from MID to the District Intelligence Officer in El Paso referred to "Cack Cobb." Problems with identifying secure informants with knowledge of Mexico may have resulted in abandonment of the program. A letter to another potential informant had found its way to the press and the program appeared under review. (MID 2338-G-180 memo of June 1, 1920, M.I.9 to Director Military Intelligence.)

29. See J. Morgan Broaddus, *The Legal Heritage of El Paso* (El Paso: Texas Western Press, 1963), 180, for information on Cobb and founding of the El Paso Bar Association.

30. See 812.00/23868 message of May 5, 1920, Cobb to State, requesting "confidential information points which I might have included in voluntary obligation from their executive to our Government." State, over the signature of the new secretary of state, Bainbridge Colby, responded the next day, "no one connected with the Department would be at liberty to advise you on the points raised in your telegram under the circumstances."

31. 812.00/24158 letter of May 17, 1920, Cobb to Colby. Cobb also made reference to Colby's stay in Chihuahua, Colby's observation of the Mexican people, and use of the code book in possession of the current collector for a reply.

32. 812.00/24158 memo of May 22, 1920, between C. M. Johnson of the Division of Mexican Affairs and W. H. Beck (NFI). See 812.00/24157 message of May 21, 1919, Cobb to State, for indications of Cobb's contacts with oil interests.

33. For inquiry on possible U.S. Marine landing at Manzanillo to protect the U.S. consulate, see 812.00/24015 message of May 18, 1920, Cobb to State. A State reply to Cobb on May 21 (same file) indicated little alarm over the situation. 812.51/587 letter of June 23, 1920, Cobb (in Washington at the time) to State, for requesting assistance in obtaining Carranza funds in New York banks. A notation on the letter reads "No action" over Mr. Johnson's initials. Cobb advised State from Los Angeles on August 20, 1920 (812.00/24480), of the allegiance of Lower California to the Mexican federal government after Pesqueira's visit with the state governor.

34. Records of the Department of State Relating to Political Relations Between the United States and Mexico, 1910–1929, Series 711.12/334, National Archives Microfilm Publication M314, letter of April 18, 1921, Cobb to State. (Hereafter cited as file number/document number.) The letter also cited legal authority for such an action.

35. 711.1211 message of May 27, 1921, Summerlin to State. This message initiated file 711.1211 and no document number was assigned. See 711.12/334 letter of April 18, 1921, Cobb to State, for internal memoranda indicating discussion of Cobb's letter.

36. See George D. Beelen, "The Harding Administration and Mexico: Diplomacy of Economic Persuasion," *The Americas* 41 (1984): 177–90 and Kenneth J. Grieb, *The Latin American Policy of Warren G. Harding* (Fort Worth: Texas Christian University Press, 1976), chap. 7, "Rapprochement with Mexico," 129–56, for a general background on diplomatic relations between the two nations under Harding. For information on the Treaty of Amity and Commerce, see Grieb, *Harding*, 134.

37. See 711.12/409 letter of March 16, 1922, U.S. consulate, Ciudad Juárez to State, for a copy of the pamphlet, and /401 letter of February 28, 1922, Governor of Arizona to President Harding.

38. 812.00/25808 letter of May 4, 1922, Cobb to State. Internal State memos and correspondence to the president are also contained in the file. Interestingly, Hughes provided the president a larger quotation from Cobb than that in Leland Harrison's earlier memo.

39. See *El Paso Times*, October 26, 1922, for announcement of Cobb's move to Los Angeles.

40. *El Paso Times*, August 7, 1921.

41. *El Paso Times*, August 9, 1921.

42. See Shawn Lay, *War, Revolution, and the Klu Klux Klan* (El Paso: Texas Western Press, 1985), 94, for the librarian's firing, and chap. 5 and 6 for details of the Klan's short-lived success in El Paso.

43. *El Paso Herald*, June 7, 1922, and Lay, *War, Revolution, and the Klu Klux Klan*, 137.

44. See Mario T. Garcia, *Desert Immigrants: The Mexicans of El Paso, 1880–1920* (New Haven: Yale University Press, 1981) chap. 8–10, and Timmons, *El*

Paso, 231–34, for the political impact of the Klan in El Paso from 1921 to 1923.

45. Both Lay, *War, Revolution, and the Klu Klux Klan,* and Gould, *Progressives and Prohibitionists,* tend to create an unbalanced racial image of Cobb.

46. See *El Paso Times,* December 21, 1951, for Cobb's association with MacAdoo and subsequent private practice.

47. See *Los Angeles Times,* December 21, 1951, for background on support of Garner and Willkie. See Senate Journal, California Legislature, Fifty-Fourth Session, 117th Calendar Day, May 2, 1941, for Cobb's speech before the California Democratic Luncheon Club and its publication for the record. Cobb also sent a copy of the speech to General Pershing. (Pershing Papers, Box 48, General Correspondence Co–Col, 1904–1948 letter of May 19, 1941, Cobb to Pershing.) For Cobb's support of Warren see *Los Angeles Times,* April 10 and 11, 1942. The articles were printed as a separate flyer supporting Warren. Cobb sent a copy of the flyer to Pershing attached to two letters dated May 13, 1942, Cobb to Pershing.

48. For Cobb-Pershing letters see Pershing Papers, Box 48, General Correspondence Co–Col, 1904–1948. Lawton is mentioned in a letter of June 25, 1941, Cobb to Pershing. Brittingham is mentioned in letters dated May 13, 1942, Cobb to Pershing; June 10, 1942, Cobb to Pershing; and June 25, 1942, Pershing to Cobb.

49. For Cobb's obituaries see *Los Angeles Times,* December 21, 1951, and *El Paso Times,* December 21, 1951. He was also a member of the Bohemian Club and the Stock Exchange Club. He was survived by his wife in Los Angeles, a brother and two sisters in Georgia, and a sister-in-law in El Paso.

B I B L I O G R A P H Y

PRIMARY SOURCES

Public Documents

National Archives and Records Administration, Washington, D.C.
    Records of the Department of State Relating to Internal Affairs of Mexico, 1910–1929, Department of State Decimal Files, Series 812. National Archives Microfilm Publication M274; General Records of the Department of State, Record Group 59.

    Records of the Department of State, Purport Lists for the Department of State Decimal File, 1910–1944, File: Department of State–Consular Code-Red; Number 119.251. National Archives Microfilm Publication M973, roll 13; General Records of the Department of State, Record Group 59.

    Records of the Department of State Relating to Internal Affairs of Germany, 1910–1929, Department of State Decimal Files, Series 862. National Archives Microfilm Publication M336, rolls 55–59; General Records of the Department of State, Record Group 59.

    Records of the Department of State, Purport Lists for the Department of State Decimal File, 1910–1944, Series 119.251, File: Administration of the U.S. Government, Organization, Function, etc.; Zachery L. Cobb, Special Agent, Department of State, Number 111.70C63/1. National Archives Microfilm Publication M973, roll 13; General Records of the Department of State, Record Group 59.

    Records of the Department of State Relating to Political Relations Between the United States and Mexico, 1910–1929, Series 711. National Archives Microfilm Publication M314; General Records of the Department of State, Record Group 59.

151

Records of the Military Intelligence Division, Record Group 165.

Records of the Bureau of Exports, Records of the Trade Division, Country File Mexico, Box 431, Record Group 182.

Records of the Adjutant General, Record Group 94.

Papers

Dallas Historical Society
    Thomas B. Love Papers

Library of Congress, Manuscript Division
    Hugh Lennox Scott Papers
    John J. Pershing Papers

Publications

Foreign Relations of the United States,1915. Washington, D.C.: U.S. Government Printing Office, 1940.
Foreign Relations of the United States, The Lansing Papers. 2 vols. Washington, D.C.: U.S. Government Printing Office, 1940.
Official Register, 1915. Washington, D.C.: U.S. Government Printing Office, 1920.

Books

Lansing, Robert. *War Memoirs of Robert Lansing, Secretary of State.* New York: Bobbs-Merrill Co., 1935.
O'Hea, Patrick. *Reminiscences of the Mexican Revolution.* Mexico City: Centro Anglo–Mexicano del Libro, 1966.
The Papers of Woodrow Wilson. Edited by Arthur S. Link. Princeton: Princeton University Press, 1966–1993.

SECONDARY SOURCES

Books

Ameringer, Charles D. *U.S. Foreign Intelligence: The Secret Side of American History.* Lexington, Conn.: Lexington Books, D.C. Heath and Co., 1990.
Anders, Evan. *Boss Rule in South Texas: The Progressive Era.* Austin: University of Texas Press, 1982.
Andrew, Christopher. *For the President's Eyes Only: Secret Intelligence and the American Presidency from Washington to Bush.* New York: HarperCollins Publishers, 1995.

Atkin, Ronald. *Revolution! Mexico 1910–1920*. New York: John Day Co., 1970.

Benjamin, Thomas, and Mark Wasserman. *Provinces of the Revolution: Essays on Regional Mexican History, 1910–1929*. Albuquerque: University of New Mexico Press, 1990.

Bozeman, Adda B. *Strategic Intelligence and Statecraft: Selected Essays*. Washington D.C.: Brassey's (U.S.), 1992.

Broaddus, J. Morgan. *The Legal Heritage of El Paso*. El Paso: Texas Western Press, 1963.

Carman, Michael Dennis. *United States Customs and the Madero Revolution*. Southwestern Studies, no. 48. El Paso: Texas Western Press, 1975.

Clendenen, Clarence C. *Blood on the Border: The United States Army and the Mexican Irregulars*. London: Macmillan Co., Collier-Macmillan Ltd., 1969.

Cobb, John E. *Cobb Chronicles*. Alexandria, Va.: Durant Publishers, 1985.

Coerver, Don M., and Linda B. Hall. *Texas and the Mexican Revolution: A Study in State and National Border Policy 1910–1920*. San Antonio: Trinity University Press, 1984.

Cumberland, Charles C. *Mexican Revolution: The Constitutionalist Years*. Austin: University of Texas Press, 1972.

Daniels, Josephus. *The Life of Woodrow Wilson 1856–1924*. Chicago: John C. Winston Co., 1924.

Dulles, Allen. *The Craft of Intelligence*. New York: Harper and Row, 1963.

Eisenhower, John S. D. *Intervention! The United States and the Mexican Revolution 1913–1917*. New York: W. W. Norton and Co., 1993.

Foote, Shelby. *The Civil War: A Narrative*. New York: Random House, 1974.

Garcia, Mario T. *Desert Immigrants: The Mexicans of El Paso, 1880–1920*. New Haven: Yale University Press, 1981.

Gilderhus, Mark T. *Diplomacy and Revolution*. Tucson: University of Arizona Press, 1977.

Gilly, Adolfo. *The Mexican Revolution*. Trans. Patrick Camiller. Thetford, Norfolk, United Kingdom: Thetford Press, 1983.

Gould, Lewis. *Progressives and Prohibitionists: Texas Democrats in the Wilson Era*. Austin: Texas State Historical Assoc., 1992.

Grieb, Kenneth J. *The Latin American Policy of Warren G. Harding*. Fort Worth: Texas Christian University Press, 1976.

Haley, Edward P. *Revolution and Intervention: The Diplomacy of Taft and Wilson with Mexico, 1910–1917*. Cambridge: Massachusetts Institute of Technology, 1970.

Hall, Kermit L., ed. *The Oxford Companion to the Supreme Court of the United States*. Oxford: Oxford University Press, 1992.

Hall, Linda B., and Don M. Coerver. *Revolution on the Border: The United States and Mexico, 1910–1920*. Albuquerque: University of New Mexico Press, 1988.

Harris, Charles H., III, and Louis R. Sadler. *The Border and the Revolution: Clandestine Activities of the Mexican Revolution: 1910–1920.* 2d ed. Silver City, N. Mex.: High-Lonesome Books, 1990.

Hart, John Mason. *Revolutionary Mexico: The Coming and Process of the Mexican Revolution.* Berkeley: University of California Press, 1987.

Hill, Larry D. *Emissaries to a Revolution: Woodrow Wilson's Executive Agents in Mexico.* Baton Rouge: Louisiana State University Press, 1973.

Jeffreys-Jones, Rhodri. *American Espionage from Secret Service to CIA.* New York: Free Press, 1977.

Johnson, William Weber. *Heroic Mexico: The Narrative History of a Twentieth Century Revolution.* Rev. ed. San Diego: Harcourt Brace Jovanovich, 1984.

Kahn, David. *The Codebreakers.* New York: Macmillan Co., 1967.

Katz, Friedrich. *The Secret War in Mexico: Europe, the United States, and the Mexican Revolution.* Chicago: University of Chicago Press, 1981.

Kerig, Dorothy Pierson. *Luther T. Ellsworth, U.S. Consul on the Border during the Mexican Revolution.* Southwestern Studies, no. 47. El Paso: Texas Western Press, 1975.

Knight, Alan. *The Mexican Revolution.* 2 vols. Cambridge: Cambridge University Press, 1986.

———. *U.S.–Mexican Relations, 1910–1940: An Interpretation.* Center for U.S.–Mexican Studies Monograph Series, no. 28. San Diego: University of California at San Diego, 1987.

Lay, Shawn. *War, Revolution, and the Ku Klux Klan: A Study of Intolerance in a Border City.* El Paso: Texas Western Press, 1985.

Machado, Manuel A., Jr. *The North Mexican Cattle Industry, 1910–1975.* College Station: Texas A&M University Press, 1981.

Meyer, Michael C. *Mexican Rebel: Pascual Orozco and the Mexican Revolution 1910–1915.* Lincoln: University of Nebraska Press, 1967.

Northern, William T. *Men of Mark in Georgia. Vol. 3, Covering the Period for 1733–1911.* Atlanta: A. B. Caldwell, 1911.

O'Toole, George J. A. *Honorable Treachery: A History of U.S. Intelligence, Espionage and Covert Action from the American Revolution to the CIA.* New York: The Atlantic Monthly Press, 1991.

Quirk, Robert E. *The Mexican Revolution 1914–1915.* Bloomington: Indiana University Press, 1960.

Simpson, John Eddins. *Howell Cobb: The Politics of Ambition.* Chicago: Adams Press, 1973.

Stuart, Graham H. *American Diplomatic and Consular Practice.* 2d ed. New York: Appleton-Century-Crofts, 1952.

Tietelbaum, Louis M. *Woodrow Wilson and the Mexican Revolution (1913–1916).* New York: Exposition Press, 1967.

Timmons, W. H. *El Paso: A Borderlands History.* El Paso: Texas Western Press, 1990.

Tuchman, Barbara. *The Zimmermann Telegram*. New York: Viking Press, 1958. Reprint, New York: Ballantine Books, 1985.

Articles

Blaisdell, Lowell L. "Henry Lane Wilson and the Overthrow of Madero." *Southwestern Social Science Quarterly* 43 (1962): 126–35.

Beelen, George D. "The Harding Administration and Mexico: Diplomacy of Economic Persuasion." *The Americas* 41 (1984): 177–90.

Clements, Kendrick A. "Woodrow Wilson's Mexican Policy, 1913–15." *Diplomatic History* 4 (Spring 1980): 113–36.

Cooper, John Milton, Jr. "'An Irony of Fate': Woodrow Wilson's Pre–World War I Diplomacy." *Diplomatic History* 3 (1980): 425–37.

Cumberland, Charles C. "Border Raids in the Lower Rio Grande Valley—1915." *Southwestern Historical Quarterly* 57 (January 1954): 285–311.

Gerlach, Allen. "Conditions along the Border–1915: The Plan de San Diego." *New Mexico Historical Review* 43 (April 1968): 195–212.

Grieb, Kenneth J. "Reginald del Valle: A California Diplomat's Sojourn in Mexico." *California Historical Society Quarterly* 47 (December 1968): 315–28.

Katz, Friedrich. "Pancho Villa and the Attack on Columbus, New Mexico." *American Historical Review* 83 (February 1978): 101–30.

Khale, Louis G. "Robert Lansing and the Recognition of Venustiano Carranza." *Hispanic American Historical Review* 38 (August 1958): 353–72.

Link, Arthur S. "The Wilson Movement in Texas, 1910–1912." *Southwestern Historical Quarterly* 48 (October 1944): 167–85.

Meyer, Michael C. "The Mexican-German Conspiracy of 1915." *The Americas* 32 (1966): 76–89.

Naylor, Thomas H. "Massacre at San Pedro de la Cueva: The Significance of Pancho Villa's Disastrous Campaign." *Western Historical Quarterly* 8 (April 1977): 127–50.

Raat, W. Dirk. "U.S. Intelligence Operations and Covert Action in Mexico, 1900–47." *Journal of Contemporary History* 22 (October 1987): 615–37.

Rausch, George J. "The Exile and Death of Victoriano Huerta." *Hispanic American Historical Review* 42 (May 1962): 133–51.

Richmond, Douglas W. "Mexican Immigration and Border Strategy during the Revolution, 1910–1920." *New Mexico Historical Review* 57 (1982): 269–88.

Sandos, James A. "German Involvement in Northern Mexico, 1915–1916: A New Look at the Columbus Raid." *Hispanic American Historical Review* 50 (February 1970): 70–78.

———. "Pancho Villa and American Security: Woodrow Wilson's Mexican Diplomacy Reconsidered." *Journal of Latin American Studies* 13 (November 1981): 293–311.

156   ZACH LAMAR COBB

Sloan, John W. "United States Policy Responses to the Mexican Revolution: A Partial Application of the Bureaucratic Politics Model." *Journal of Latin American Studies* 10 (November 1978): 255–71.

Interviews

Marshall, S. L. A. Interview by Richard Estrada. University of Texas at El Paso, Institute of Oral History, July 7–19, 1975.

Unpublished Thesis

Estrada, Richard Medina. "Border Revolution: The Mexican Revolution in Cuidad Juárez–El Paso Area, 1906–1915." Master's Thesis, University of Texas at El Paso, 1975.

Newspapers

El Paso Herald
El Paso Morning Times
El Paso Times
Los Angeles Times
New York Times